LAUGHTER ON
THE BUS

Random Jaunts
Around the Americas

By

Geoffrey Leo

About the Author

Born and bred in Wolverhampton from mixed Suffolk and Italian stock, Geoffrey Leo has spent a career as ice cream man, entrepreneur and teacher.

He plays rugby and golf, and is husband to Karen. They live on Cannock Chase and enjoy walking their dog, Glen, riding their horses, Rosie and Taffie, and share their love of the forest, its wildlife and great open spaces with their eight grandchildren.

As he first travelled Europe before going off-continent, Geoff has been plagued in much the same way as taxi drivers (Been busy?, When's your shift end?) with the stock question asked of teachers everywhere, "What do you teach?" Apparently pausing for thought he grins and answers "Little B*****ds!" and the ice has been broken with everyone except Americans who have no idea of the concept of irony.

If you must ask; Maths, English, Humanities and Business Studies

Author's Note

With a generous teacher's pension and a legacy from the Leo's family ice cream business I feel I am able to donate any profits made from this trilogy to Compton Care, a hospice based in Wolverhampton. My thanks to Cyril Barrett from the Talbot for suggesting this worthwhile charity.

For

Spencer and Phoebe

A Time Capsule

Contents:

Acknowledgements

I'd like to thank all of the people and organisations I have travelled with and have apparently always conveyed me to where I was supposed to be going, safely. I'd also like to thank the people who have provided me with a fund of anecdotes and stories I have included here. Most importantly, I must thank Kaz, my long suffering partner, who has complained bitterly about my incessant adventures, but has supported me all the way with patience and a good deal of understanding. I thank Cyril Barrett for suggested sponsoring Compton Care, a worthy charity. Finally, Sam Roden; friend, colleague and now editor, for her unfailing professionalism.

South of Texas, most people in most places use local transport to commute. There are mules and donkeys, mopeds and tri-peds, trucks and beat up mini-buses, and the most popular, chicken buses. These are usually second hand school buses sent from the USA. They are decorated and mercilessly pimped with chrome and Christian symbols. Rosaries and Jesus and Mary statues are fixed everywhere. They are called chicken buses because people transport all their worldly good on them, including livestock. They are always packed and noisy, with happy chatter and loads of laughter. Totally different to our solemn commute experience.

It is this simple sense of enjoyment of life which stays with you. Poverty and hardship is as nothing. So I thank all the people I've been crushed together with on these buses. I thank them for all the

LAUGHTER ON THE BUS

Prologue

My first trip abroad was with my parents and elder brother to Viareggio, the up-market beach resort for contemporary Romans, when I was seven. Flights from Luton to Milan with Swan Tours, then by train to our hotel, and we were there during the Rome Olympics of 1960. My brother taught me to swim by holding my head under water, and I hated the food. Mum continually fretted while Dad was forever imploring the kindly waiters for "Grapianos", the only things I'd eat: grapes.

In secondary school, at 12, I joined Mr Darby's trip to Souillac in the Dordogne. Ferry to Dieppe and overnight train through France. Mr Darby was my favourite teacher, French my favourite subject, and I've been a Francophile ever since. Paris is still my favourite city.

The Beatles' Eight Days A Week was on the juke box in the Salle Des Jeunes every night where we played baby-foot (table football) and smuggled in cheap wine which I proceeded to line the toilet with; to this day I still can't drink Sauternes, the smell is enough to put me off. I learned all about mammoths, cave drawings, and kissing girls.

Later that summer I went camping in St Tropez with the folks, before Brigitte Bardot made it chic.

In 1969, before Christmas, just following our mock 'O' Levels, I went on a school cruise on the HMS Uganda, later to be used as a hospital ship during the Falklands conflict. We flew to Venice which we explored whilst waiting for schools from all over Britain to join the ship. We set sail for Piraeus and Athens; then past Gallipoli, through the Sea of Marmara and to the Bosphoros, and on to Istanbul; next stop Crete's Heraklion; then all the way to the western Mediterranean and Gibraltar; finally crossing the Bay of Biscay and disembarking at Southampton. St Mark's Square, The Parthenon, The Blue Mosque, The Palace at Knossos, Barbary Apes; I was hooked, and my future mapped. That whole trip cost an unbelievable £59.

In my twenties as I built my career and began to climb the property ladder. I married and, as was the fashion, took package holidays to the Spanish Costas and the Balearics . Later, after my first divorce, I explored the Greek Islands and rediscovered France; Normandy, Brittany, La Vendee and the Languedoc, one of my favourite areas to explore in the world are the foothills of the Pyrenees just west of Perpignan, so much Cathar history, Languedoc cuisine, Mediterranean light.

I became a teacher and led many educational trips and exchanges to Paris, Barcelona, Rome, Hanover, Amsterdam and Athens again. There was a downside, endless days in Disneyland, Paris.

Turkey became a favourite for family holidays, and instead of being packaged, I was beginning to explore; island-hopping, planning journeys using local transport from town to city, and walking and trekking on then off trails, and along hills and into deserts and conquering mountains.

Into Africa and Morocco (The Marrakesh Express to Casablanca used post war British Rail rolling stock!) and Tunisia; then the jewel that is Egypt and its ancient civilisations, and moving away from the Mediterranean into the coral wonders of the Red Sea, North to Lawrence's Aqaba and the wonder of the Nabatean's Petra. I discovered glorious snorkelling over reefs and thought it was the best thing, until my first visit to Kenya and the sheer joy and excitement of safari. I did ten before I saw a cat (some accused me of being a Jonah), but it is the exhilaration of the search, and spotting so many other wonderful animals. You would do it all just for the antelope, elephant and giraffe.

I took my daughter to Barbados and on a Mediterranean cruise. She has inherited my wanderlust and became a travel executive. I went further afield and wept when I saw the Taj Mahal, marvelled at the heroes that built the Thai-Burma Railway, braved the Inca trail to Machu Pichu and gazed with wonder at both the Grand Canyon and Iguazu Falls. I've swum with dolphins, bathed elephants, stroked cheetahs and crocodiles, sat with gorillas and ridden an ostrich. But with these surreal experiences came all manner of scrapes, traumas and near-misses.

I marooned the family on the river Aude after capsizing, and left them in the middle of a forest fire in Spain. I nearly fell off Victoria Falls, was 'taken out' by a police officer on Key West, and have been arrested as a suspected gun runner in Ethiopia. I swam across the Akanan river in Venezuela to free a stranded boat, and I've dived in to rescue Russian tourists in distress. I've been charged by elephants, chased by monkeys, attacked by trigger fish and had my nose bitten by a toucan. I've slept on beaches, in parks, in railway stations, airports and on mountains (but mainly in hotels, I'm no Bear Grylls). And through all this my constant companions have been Bill Bryson, Stephen Fry, and a host of other travel writers, occasionally Tolstoy, and my own trusty travelogue, written up religiously (well almost) every night whilst nursing a well-earned, and very cold, beer or two.

I've become so adept at gallivanting that I now get itchy feet if I spend more than one night in any location, what I call my One-Night Stands. The constant moving on and episodes of solitude can sometimes bring on self-pitying bouts of home sickness, and I've often returned home declaring never again. Only to begin planning my next trip within weeks. There are family holidays in between of course, but they prefer the beach, the pool, theme parks, and all-inclusive luxury. Not much room for crusades, 'tilting at windmills' or indeed misadventure there, nor even gallivanting, apparently my favourite pastime.

Introduction

It hit me. As I was seated on the south shore of Ometeppe Island in Lake Nicaragua, looking out on the sunset which silhouetted the mountains and volcanoes on the opposite shore. To my left, a willow tree wept its branches into the water with dozens of snowy white egrets roosting upright. I was listening to a family of howler monkeys cavorting and grunting their way through a copse of flowering trees behind and to a singing tree full of tiny finches to my right. In front, a piebald farm horse rested its weary legs up to its haunches in the calm, warm waters of the lake which were gradually turning every hue of red. I was contemplating beginning my return journey the next day, ending another episode of random jaunts, and I thought of being homeward bound.

I was singing softly to myself, Paul Simon's Homeward Bound, the first record I ever bought, a vinyl 45, sometime in the mid-sixties, when I was a mere love-struck teenager.

"That's apt," I thought, my other self simultaneously wondering what a strange word "apt" was, then thinking, "well what's the Spanish for apt anyway? I'll google it. That's how my thoughts wander, escaping.

Like Paul, I have spent hours sitting in railway stations, bus stations, airports, then having finally started the journey you realise there are still hours to go before you reach your first destination. Unlike him, I am no wandering troubadour, poet or folk singer, gigging around the country. I am merely a visitor, an observer, a one-man band of another ilk, randomly using locations as stepping stones. Strangers' faces that I see are opportunities to explore strange new worlds, discover foreign lands, seek out new civilisations, and hopefully kindle fresh friendships. To boldly go, splitting the infinitive.

Homeward Bound refers to visiting movies and factories, smoking cigarettes and reading magazines. Well for me it is usually a good book, and cigarettes went out the window years ago. If I went to the cinema I probably wouldn't understand the films, or they are dubbed instead of sub-titled. ("Bonjour!" I once heard a gruff voice say from the television in a hotel room in Paris whilst I showered; "Je m'appelle Captain Kirk, et J'ai le plaisir de vous presente Monsieur Spock!". Another time I saw Verdi's Rigoletto in Madrid, and it was sung in Italian with Spanish subtitles above the stage. I found it very difficult to not try to translate the Spanish, and couldn't keep my eyes off the moving words! I did go to a cinema once, whilst sailing the ferry from Portsmouth to Bilbao. I wanted to see A Fish Called Wanda, but when the auditorium darkened and the credits came up, I knew the title "Cuatro Bodas y un Funeral" meant I'd entered the wrong door. I swiftly got up and left Hugh Grant to it.)

Paul, a New Yorker, was gigging around Northern English towns, when he penned what would become his second British hit, sung with Art Garfunkel. I was born and brought up a little further south, in the Black Country, cradle of the industrial revolution, all dark, satanic mills, apparently. I have to admit, I love my home, but I yearn for the exotic; to cross oceans and visit distant shores, the wonders of the world, both natural and man made. I have that wanderlust.

But there is the prospect of being homeward bound. This is never far from my thoughts, as my odysseys have to be short bites. This is because the love waiting for me is rather vociferous in her opposition to my travels. In my mind I'm on expeditions, exploring, seeking adventure, researching; boldly going... But to Karen they are simply holidays and I am merely a hapless tourist; gallivanting.

So that's when it hit me, Random Thoughts, Random Jaunts. My first set of Random Jaunts is around the Americas, and we begin right in the middle, on the bracelet that joins North to South; Panama.
("Es oportuno", Spanish for apt).

Panama: from Coast to Coast

It is estimated over 27,000 people died constructing the Panama Canal. Many were white people succumbing to tropical diseases, but mostly the victims were Indians perishing from the diseases introduced by the white man.

As a 10-year-old, I remember a lesson at school about the two great canals (Suez and Panama) and seeing a picture in a text book of a ship in a lock, then the lock with the ship having left. With some urgency I threw up my hand and asked the teacher why the water level hadn't changed. (I like to think that I was bringing into play the Archimedes Principle, but of course, I wasn't. I was just being a smart Alec). Mr Halstead wiped the floor with me, explaining disdainfully that the locks were so huge the entrance and exit of one ship would have no effect on the displacement of water. He was obviously pleased with his performance and clapped and rubbed his hands, Basil-Fawlty-like in satisfaction. He had me almost in tears. I decided then, in that precise moment, that I'd visit the canal – something Halstead, the old stiff, would never have the inclination to do.

For some strange reason that particular put-down stayed with me, and – whilst it took me nearly 50 years – I stayed true to my juvenile conviction. It transpires that in less than a century since its construction the land is no longer ravaged by disease, but graced with birds and butterflies and beautiful people, the antithesis of Mr Halstead. I suppose I should thank him, but I wouldn't, even if I could.

Panama City

My visit began with a flight from Birmingham to Amsterdam. The descent into Schiphol was memorable for it was a lovely, sunny day. We flew low, over regimented fields of red, yellow and blue tulips, fringed by straight, straight roads and canals. At Schiphol I underwent a free health check standing on one of those "I speak your weight" machines. My BMI was above average (put it down to muscle), but more worryingly, so was my blood pressure. I needed to relax, and a long flight over the Atlantic was the perfect remedy.

At Tocumen airport I was met by Nicolas from GoPanama, the company I had engaged to organise my itinerary. Nicolas was unlike any travel courier I'd encountered; a handsome, young Hispanic with sneakers, faded jeans and a white tee shirt, which didn't even say 'Go Panama' on it. He drove me, in a rather beat-up Renault Clio, through a downpour in the dark into a vast sky-scrapered city to a rather seedy hostel where I was checked into a dormitory: my ten-year-old self might have felt at home, but my slightly rotund, slightly anxious current self - felt annoyed that I wouldn't be able to sleep in my boxer shorts without an audience observing my paunch. "I will pick you up after breakfast for your flight to David", Nicolas confirmed, handing me my backpack.

I eventually took to my bed about 10:30, which was 4:30am UK time, after some cold beers. I had spent the evening chatting to a thirty-something Twickenham couple who are "doing" the Americas in three months. Both barristers – Abby and Stuart from Lichfield, with its three-steepled cathedral and the birthplace of Dr Johnston: only ten miles from where I live! They are waiting for a passage to Colombia.

The dormitory was comfortable, but I awoke at 2:30. I couldn't put a light on so I just reclined I showered and cooked breakfast from the pancake mixture supplied - pouring salt over it from the sugar dispenser! So much for my blood pressure - and stepped outside into the steaming hot morning for an orientation stroll.

My first impressions were of rubbish strewn streets (like

many developing cities, black bags are put out by shops and businesses, and are rummaged overnight by dogs, cats and the homeless) but there were immaculate schoolchildren. There was the usual profusion of cars and taxis, but most apparent were the choking fumes from overcrowded 2nd hand U.S. buses, called "Red Devils", and the scurrying workers hurrying off and onto those same buses clutching coffees and churros bought at the kerbside. Indian, Spanish, brown, white: all blended together. In amongst the pot-holed roads, high leg-breaking kerbs and storm drains big enough to swallow you whole, there was the strange juxtaposition of modern skyscrapers springing up from the crumbling and dirty facades of colonial style buildings; many bordering on dilapidated. But there were also landscaped parks with grassy knolls and ancient wide, shade giving trees. At this time of day though, there was no one relaxing under those huge boughs: it was all scamper.

The fun starts back at the hostel. There is a message. No transfer to airport...make own way in taxi...GoPanama to reimburse. Here we go, I thought, ruefully. Nicolas did turn up however, saying the car was giving him a little trouble, and stopped me from having to endure a rant from a red-faced expat Brit who the world had ripped off. "Costa Rica, Cuba; just don't go there. Too much dog mess. Brighton is just too gay. Taxation to the hilt, I say, taxation to the hilt!" I just swung in my hammock, waiting for Nicolas to take me to the airport for my flight to David.

Boquette, Chiriqui

Following my orientation walk and Nicolas' will-he-won't-he pickup, there was a picturesque if noisy one-hour flight into the tiny David airport. I was met by Sergio, a short, stocky thirty-something with a battered straw hat who drove me to Boquete and will pick me back up in two days. As I arrived in the small provincial town there was a lively fiesta and carnival marking the town's centenary. All of the children were costumed, and most appeared to be banging drums or blowing tuneless trumpets. I checked into the Mamaleena Hostel on the plaza and eventually decided on my afternoon activity. I was one day into the trip and already on Plan C. It was incredibly frustrating that my original intention had been to climb the highest point in Panama, the Volcan Baru, but there was no guide available for my three days here. Plan B had been to experience the white water rafting for which the town was famous, but a group had already left and the trip didn't run the following day. So what was left was an invigorating solo trek along the Caldera River valley, up to the San Ramon waterfall.

I kitted myself out for the long walk, or so I thought. So many mistakes, indicative of the fact that I was still a little disoriented with the time difference: I jettisoned my padlock for weight, forgetting I was in a hostal dormitory; I left my plastic poncho in the room – in a rainforest; I wore nylon socks with my boots– hot and tight on already swollen ankles, courtesy of the long flight; I left my towel on the washing line – always carry it to wipe away sweat; I didn't empty my rucksack and therefore carried three heavy books; I walked in swimming shorts – nylon gusset, result: an unbearably sore groin.

The walk itself followed the path of the ever rushing Caldera river; its roar sometimes deafening. Up and up into the cloud forest. Lovely views, beautiful flora, wonderful trees and bromeliads, although the daturas (trumpet flowers) were a week past their best. There were many beautiful birds; motmots, tanagers, trogons and honeycreepers, the occasional hummingbird and colourful butterflies, and fascinating leaf-cutting ants are everywhere. Overall it was a gruelling if uneventful adventure, with a pretty, multi-step waterfall halfway up. A five-hour round trip.

Caldera Hot Springs

After dinner I chatted with two Swedish women who were (I hadn't realised) my room mates. Dark haired Petra had welts at the top of her legs caused by sitting on narrow seating when white-water rafting, which she insisted on showing me. She lifted her shorts to expose the bottom of her buttocks. I laughed nervously. "It's O.K." she explained "My dad's a Jordanian doctor!"

Later that evening I met Dave. David (pronounced Daveed, same as the airport), was from Austria, a lovely, friendly young man with a shy grin and curly blond hair, wearing a safari suit and floppy hat. He speaks confident if broken English with a double lisp, as in "I'm fwom Thaltthburg, Authtwia".

Up at 6:30, I cooked the perfect pancake (with sugar this time), chatted in the kitchen and pottered until catching the 10:45 bus, with Dave, to the Caldera hot springs. Caldera derives from 'cauldron', so you would expect hot springs. After the bus there was a 45-minute walk to the pools which was scenic and moderately difficult. We eventually came upon an Indian farm house with ducks, geese and turkeys; horses and goats; beyond were the springs.

There were three pools to choose from. The two in the upper meadow were hot and overhung with jungle; very cobwebby, and there was one down by the river besides which we lunched. I tried to swim in the river but it was too cold, then returned to the pools in the upper meadow and snoozed in the sunshine. I woke to see Dave being followed by a juvenile spider monkey who saw me and decided I was its mother. He loped towards me and leapt into my arms (the monkey, not Dave). My first reaction was to flinch away. After all, it was a monkey, it could bite. But he clung and cuddled affectionately. He held me tight with both arms, both legs, and his prehensile tail, the end of which was just like a huge finger. He was clamped to me. It was a magical few minutes. The only way Cheetah would move from me was when I took him to the little Indian girl from the farmhouse whose pet he turned out to be.

Next we set off for home via the hydroelectric dam. We came upon an idling pick-up truck and quick as a flash Dave is up and on the rear bed, he hauls me up to join him and we're off down the dirt track leading to the main road back to Boquete. A rollercoaster ride on rutted roads. The sides of the truck were beaten up, rusted and jagged, we shared the bed with more scrap metal. Had we over balanced when hitting a pothole, we could have sliced whole chunks off ourselves. We waved cheerfully as we passed a couple of miserable looking cyclists and people who were waiting for the bus, as if to say, "So long, suckers!", then we were dropped off. I was still wondering which bus stop to stand at when Dave spotted a taxi containing the two disaffected cyclists. Suddenly, we're in the taxi, squeezed up alongside them. Half an hour later we're back in Boquete. I tried to pay the taxi, but Dave's beaten me to it. That's why I felt obligated to buy him a couple of beers. He is "thwee monthth into a year'th twip awound the Amewicath" and is yet to leave Panama.

Abby and Stuart (from Twickenham) have turned up. They have been on a bus all day and at one stage were held up (not literally) for three hours because of a protest march. They can't get a boat to Colombia for at least two weeks so have come up to Chiriqui. We chatted late into the night but Dave didn't join us. He's quite shy: a one Englishman at a time sort of guy.

Bocas Town on the Isla Colon

Up at 5:30, Sergio collected me to drive to the Sentera Canabra. We embarked on a bird watching trek (with lots of "Shushh!", looking up, "See, in the green tree!" (they're all green) and much stationary time, or consulting the guide - a book, not Sergio/. It's always damp and fresh in the cloud forest, with abundant vegetation, but not much colour; trees festooned with bromeliads, and weird and wonderful birdsong. Lots of small creepers, warblers and finches and many colourful magpie sized birds, but the highlight was a male quetzal; very spectacular with a long multi coloured tail. On our descent we saw the only other person we had encountered all morning, an Indian with a rucksack with a barrel sticking out. "Why did he have a rifle?" I asked Sergio. "In case of puma attack" he replied. "Where's ours?" I asked. He didn't reply.

Sergio brought me back to the Mamaleena Hostal and we took an early burger lunch together before his brother Ernesto picked me up for the transfer, north to the Bocas de Toro archipelago on the Caribbean Sea. The three-hour journey in a people carrier (and I was the only person) took us across the continental divide. Ernesto explained in his excellent English as we drove through the pass, that up to this point, all rivers flow into the Pacific, and from here on, all rivers flow into the Atlantic, hence the Divide. At the coastal town of Almirante, Ernesto organised a water taxi which sped me on an exhilarating half hour passage past mangrove islands over a silver blue flat sea to Bocas Town. I have to make my own way to the brightly painted Hostal Gran Kahuna, a whole 30 yards.

As soon as I dumped my bags I was keen to snorkel and asked Venus on the desk where I might find the best coral reef. "Donde es el mejor arrecife de coral?" She is a beautiful, tall afro-american girl who recommended - in perfect English - that I try Hospital Point. So, kitted up with fins and mask (carrying, not wearing) I walked to the jetty opposite and summoned another water taxi for the $7 trip. After a short journey I am deposited in a tiny cove which has only a 6-foot fringe of beach backed by an impenetrable spider infested jungle. Back at six, I agree with the boatman.

The coral is adequate, with lots of old friends: wrasses, groupers, butterflies, angels, surgeons, sergeant-majors, tangs, etc., but nothing special or spectacular except for an impressive green moray eel which swung its huge tooth filled jaws menacingly from its lair, but it is harmless.

Among my favourite reef fish are grunts. They are a pretty fish, not unlike dories, yellow with black spots, often found shoaling around coral reefs, so why they have such an unfortunate handle is hard to understand. To compound this, there is a variety to be found off the Canary Islands called a 'bastard grunt'. How on earth can you gain such an awful nomenclature?

Back and forth I snorkelled, exhausting the whole cove, and beyond, but wary of meeting a current which could take me too far around the headland. Finally, I decided 6 o'clock must be approaching, and leave the water and wait, drying off in the weakened rays of the sun as it drifts lower in the western sky. And I wait, and wait, and then begin to feel anxious. Worrying is futile when the circumstances are beyond one's control, I know, but I am totally alone on this tiny beach on this tiny island, with nowhere to go if the boatman forsakes me and Venus forgets me, and thoughts of the film Open Water begin to unnerve me. Stranded at the mercy of the sea...But I'm on land, idiot.

Anyway, he arrived. Albeit with the sun having all but disappeared, but he arrived.

On my return from Hospital Point, I met up with three lads from Ipswich (Tractor Boys, they called themselves) and their girlfriends for drinks and chatted on the Gran Kahuna balcony, cooked myself cheesy pasta and found myself the only occupant of a six berth dorm.

Zapatillas Islands

Up early to experience dawn on this laid back, one street, colourful, musical resort, I breakfasted on beans and coffee, then I was picked up for my pre-booked boat trip around the islands. I shared the boat with two young couples from Albuquerque, New Mexico; a couple of ladies from Florida and two Canadians; Amy with a broken leg, Frank, originally from Bolton, Lancashire.

We set off from the quay after fuelling up, and the late arrival of the Canadian couple, but were soon skimming across a flat blue sea making introductions. First to Dolphin Bay, and although we could see a school leaping in the distance, we entered some mangrove fringed lagoons and arrived at a sheltered area to spend half an hour with several bottlenose dolphins who simply circled, only breaking the surface to breath. Maybe it was a crèche area, but certainly very subdued. However, as promised in the publicity blurb, we had seen these beautiful creatures, for plastered Amy, who was in advertising. The ladies from Florida wondered what all the fuss was about! From these quiet lagoons we sped off to Cabo Cay for a loo break, to order lunch and snorkel. This was an open water dive and there was an abundance of attractive plant life, but few fish. "What did you see?" asked Wayne, the fire fighter. "A lot of good shit," replied Frank, a bar manager. Succinct, but apt, I thought.

The fish lunch was expensive, and only adequate, however the location, in the middle of the ocean was beautiful and the chat, enjoyable. Politics and Obama, current affairs, life in Alaska (Palin can see Russia which, she says, qualifies her for Presidency) and Kansas; one town was officially designated the Land of Oz, and all the Munchkins visited. We discussed canvassing for Obama in red neck Missouri; Senate debates: "The Republicans just filibuster any of Barack's attempted reforms", complained Naomi, a nurse; British PMQ's (They are fascinated by our Prime Minister's Questions (wow, intelligent and knowledgeable Americans!); the National Health Service; Churchill's great quotes, and much more. This, of course, was BT; before Trump. I wonder how they're getting along now.

We then departed for one of the twin Zapatillas islands. An Indian National Park. One of the most beautifully archetypal little desert islands imaginable, this was just pristine white beach and palm trees. It is a turtle nesting sanctuary, hence the shallow sloping sandy approach, which may be perfect for turtles but makes it poor for snorkelling: no coral reef. I tried three dive sites, and walked the half mile through the middle of the island, past a research post where I was chased by a dog, to its north coast while everyone else just sunbathed. Then the long journey home into the sunset.

It was a great pity the evening was a write off. Couple of beers, spoke briefly to the Tractor Boys, snoozed in the hammock, cooked potatoes, onions and pineapple in paprika. "What's that?" enquired Tractor Boy #1, "Some good shit" I replied.

Boca Del Drago

I am seated on a bus outside the tiny Bocas Town square, under a huge banyan tree, waiting, waiting. Typical Caribbean Mañana. Wait for bus; bus arrives; get on bus; driver gets off and disappears. I am apparently going to Drago where a boat can take me to Starfish Beach.

The driver re-emerges, and the bus begins to fill up, lots of chatter and laughter. Eventually we depart – a lovely ride, 10 miles through pristine (except for the pitted road) rainforest, stopping occasionally to pick up or drop off locals, collect groceries, make postal deliveries, or sometimes for no apparent reason. I arrived at this amazingly unspoilt, palm-fringed strip of land and trekked (instead of taking the boat) through the mangrove and dune forest to Starfish Beach. It is well named. All of them are colourfully patterned, at least a foot across, and in one place where I paddled, I counted over 30 huge starfish, and a large conch shell, its inhabitant walking across the sand. But the sea was unusually cool. In the dune forest were pigs, lizards, soldier crabs and insects, and the biggest bright blue butterfly I've ever seen.

After a much better lunch, red snapper with rice and beans, I snorkel the Boca Del Drago reef, and indeed, as I had read, it is severely damaged. A good experience for the novice, but less than 10% of the variety of life found, say in the Red Sea. I snooze in a hammock (is there a better way?) then take the bus ride home again; fascinating, especially with the scattered Indian homes with children playing in the dirt, eccentric Episcopal churches, and the clapperboard Caribbean colourful cabins. All porches must have a hammock and a rocking chair. I shower and change at the Gran Kahuna, then take a $1 taxi to the airport where there are at least 250 boys playing football at the end of the runway.

The Full Transit

The internal flight took less than an hour back to Tocumen. But the luggage pick up was hilarious. Everyone (there were perhaps a dozen passengers) was given a raffle ticket on departure, and on landing we had to stand behind a barrier, and an official stood with our baggage. Only when your raffle ticket was called were you allowed to step forward and collect your luggage. I nearly shook his hand and thanked him for my prize, but they take themselves so seriously, these officials.

Nicolas met me ("The car is with the mechanic!") from the airport and we went by taxi to my new, posh but soulless Hostal Amador near the Causeway which joins the city to Flamenco Island. "I will see you mañana mañana" Nicolas assured and he popped back into the taxi and sped off.

In the kitchen I chatted with Avan, a very large man, who was cooking octopus and explaining how to do it properly. He was from Venezuela and had escaped the Hugo Chavez regime to live in Miami and was now visiting Panama with his son Junior, a really handsome Hispanic twenty something. We had a couple of beers, I cooked pasta with red wine, drank the rest of the wine, read Stephen Fry, and took to my bed.

I was up at six, excited, for today is the "Full Transit", the highlight of the whole adventure. I showered, rushed breakfast and waited in the lobby for Nico's 6:45 collection. Nothing! And I have no way of contacting him or Natasha at GoPanama. This Hostal does not have a working computer, and the documents I have from Natasha bear the wrong phone number. I can only wait. But with 7:30 approaching and boat departure supposedly at 7:15! I am beginning to panic. I know; Junior has his IPhone. He is taking his breakfast and I interrupt. He quickly finds GoPanama's number, rings Natasha and there is a heated, garbled conversation, which he assured me later included a lot of expletives.

"Follow me" Junior instructed. Out to his car we ran for the drive to the quay. It was ten minutes of tyres squealing and sharp cornering, but when we arrived there was a ship waiting.

"Señor Leo from GoPanama? Welcome aboard", and the immaculate young lady at her lectern indicated I should take the gangplank. I turned to thank Junior but he was gone, and as soon as I came aboard so the ship slipped her moorings.

I was on board the Pacific Princess with 250 others, about to transit from Pacific to Atlantic. Everyone is fitted with wristbands to indicate full (to Colon) or half (to Balboa) transit, and sittings for breakfast, lunch and snacks. There is commentary throughout in English and Spanish, and then, belatedly in German as we had a coach party on board. The ship is fairly crowded as we leave the key, and circle North to face the first of the Panama Canal locks, and true to type the Germans have spread towels, bags and coats on all the best forward seating. This is of course impossible as there needs to be fluidity and movement about the ship, but Germans will be Germans, and in the absence of sunbeds…

The canal is a spectacular, costly, but superb feat of early 20th century engineering. The design and operation of the locks alone are admirable. All the sets of lock gates were built and riveted to the same specification as the Titanic, and they all still existed without having needed any repairs or modifications. Over 100 years old. Mind you, icebergs have never attempted the transit.

We entered the first lock and watched the water slowly rise to the next level and we are released up into the second lock. Behind us we can see an incredible number of ships dotted around the Pacific bay, awaiting instructions to proceed.

Two sets of locks take us up to Lake Miraflores and we wave to all the sightseers from the specially built visitor centre and museum, then into the third lock which takes us up to Lake Gatun, 85 feet above sea level "the same for both oceans, that's why it's called sea level" explained the commentary, with just a hint of irony. Half the passengers leave after lunch at Balboa, and we continue along Lake Gatun which is really the Chagres river valley, dug out by hand and flooded over a century ago. The islands we pass now were the hilltops then that all the wildlife fled to. This artificial concentration of creatures proved perfect for the Smithsonian Institute to study and make detailed descriptions of the area's flora and fauna. The water is green, reflecting the rainforest banks, and is sometimes over a mile wide.

We pass huge ships, carrying up to 5,000 containers, so incongruous, inland. I chat at length to Dennis from Tasmania, who has over 80 countries under his belt, (this prompts me to count up my record: just 50), and to Brian from Zimbabwe who works out of Dallas for Tetrapack and is on a day off from his business trip.

There are more Americans on the transit than any other nationality, and one guy latches onto the fact I am English, and therefore European, and asks "Is it true that Germans are the ugly Americans of Europe?" "I wouldn't describe them as American!" I quipped, which prompts a discussion about silly EU rules and 'Elf 'n' Safety' with which the press from both sides of the pond appear fixated.

I encountered three mature American ladies, one from Nebraska. "Am I right in saying Omaha is your state capital?" I asked. "Why, yes it is, it is my home town, unfortunately famous for nothing". "Er! The D-Day beach?" I opined. "I thought it was a ship" she offered. "Quite so" I confirmed.

What does the Panama Canal achieve? The commentary was very informative. Shipping companies pay a small fortune to use it, which is why Panama is much wealthier than its neighbours. It saves weeks, and is much safer than the journey around Cape Horn, so there is less wear and tear, goods are transported quicker, and cargoes can include perishables, but mostly it saves a fortune on fuel. Could we build it today? Well they e are having to rebuild the locks because the Chinese are intent on building bigger and bigger boats.

On the bridge we listen to the pilot instructing the captain in English, and with the captain giving the commentary in English, I asked the obvious question, "It is the international maritime language?" He explains, "You cannot become an officer on any ship unless you can speak English."

We descend the three locks down into the Caribbean and Atlantic, and dock at Colon. At the final lock there is a huge flock of pelicans perched on the gates and dock sides, and both turkey-vultures and frigate birds circling above. The reason being that the locks are filled with fresh water from Lake Gatun. This is then spilled into the salty ocean, killing the freshwater fish unfortunate enough to have been trapped. Hence the bird feast.

Out in the ocean are dozens of ships awaiting their transit. We've done ours, and there is cheering as this fact is broadcast. My personal disembarkation instructions are announced over the tannoy, a nice, individualised touch, I thought, and we are bussed the 60 or so miles back to Panama.

I am dropped off outside my hostel, which is empty except for a bearded American in my dorm who champions the virtues of must-visit Easter Island and Burma. Hardly next door to each other, but it always prompts the question, "Where next?" We had also bemoaned all the failed enterprises which appear to litter Panama (and many other parts of the world since the Credit Crunch of 2008); I'd seen abandoned theme parks, half built hotels, and many decaying adventure lands. Each failed enterprise a shattered dream and broken heart.

I've spoken to Natasha and tomorrow I'm taking the bus. About this morning's confusion? She assured me my driver had waited outside for 15 minutes. Right, of course.

El Valle De Anton

I have come to the Garden of Eden that is El Valle De Anton. Everyone refers to it as just The Valley. Downside? It is as quiet as the grave. My hostel, (own room, en-suite, woo-hoo!) on the outskirts, called Cariguana, is not for backpackers. Therefore, there is no kitchen, no communal lounge, no bar, no company! Last night had been the same anyway, Avan and Junior having left. I really felt guilty I hadn't the chance to thank Junior for his help. I had a bit of a chat with beard, read Fry in the hammock in the garden, drank wine and wandered out for a late night pizza.

I had woken early, breakfasted well, packed and hailed a taxi for The Terminal. There is only one, and it includes the bus depot, railway station and domestic airport (how enlightened). I bought a ticket and found the Valley bus. I was the 25th on a 25 seater, and the object of much curiosity. Since my first observations, I have concluded that 90% of the population are

Indian, most of whom trace to local tribes. They probably own less than 1% of the wealth. I've also observed that most young girls have a babe in arms or at the breast. Officially about 70% are Mestizo, which is a mix of Amerindian and white, the rest being either pure Indian or black, the descendants of African slaves.

Back to the bus. A bumpy ride, also accompanied throughout by loud merengue and salsa music, and much laughter, mostly aimed at me, I thought. We wind gradually up into the hills, agriculture all around, through a pass then slowly down into this sheltered verdant valley. After two hours of being bounced around and stared at, I alight into a very busy market street. I take a taxi to the Cariguana to meet Esteban, a silver haired, camp, and very dapper 55-year-old. He introduced me to his two aunts in their 80's and his 102-year-old grandmother. She asks how I am. "Muy bien, gracias, y usted?" She mutters something to Esteban which was probably "What the gringo say?"

"She is into medical plans" he says. I am wondering who would insure her, when he hands me a crushed leaf, "This plan is very good for the liver…" (Oh! *Plants*) and he gives me a tour of his garden, and picks for me the sweetest mango I have ever tasted (and shows me how to properly eat them; biting the bottom point and peeling down with the teeth) "from the shape, we call these old-woman's-breasts." Certainly firm, sweet and succulent. Probably something of an oxymoron.

I take lunch in the town; chorizo, rice and pasta, and set off on my afternoon trek. A mistake. I head up into the cloud forest and it is too similar to Boquete, although I do see a tiny green humming bird: beautiful, and always a favourite to tick off. I climb higher and higher and take a couple of false trails before realising there is no loop, and head back down. Throughout the trek there were wonderful views of the valley, which is an ancient crater surrounded by the insides of a colossal volcano; and many gorgeous butterflies and birds. Returning to the valley floor, with its wondrous flora, I decided no climbing tomorrow, I would explore the town's surroundings, when toucans will be on my wish list.

Nightfall brings a cacophony of frog calls, rhythmic squeaks and hoots, plus myriad fireflies. I walked up the leafy lane, back into town to find a bar. The frogs are going at it hammer and tongs. "Boop, beep, hoot…" Even when crouched right over the noise, shining my headtorch into the undergrowth, I couldn't see them. I found Ty's Canadian Bar. Over a couple of beers, I watched the ice hockey. The menu looked so good, and the Canadian couple I met gushed so enthusiastically about their meal, that I resolved to return tomorrow for dinner. I weaved my way home, and being rather late, the bars - which are just doors in buildings, no fancy frontage, windows, or signs - are spilling out drunken locals, both men and women, much the same as at home, either loudly declaring their undying love for one another, or spoiling for a fight.

I woke at dawn and walked to some hot springs, birdwatching. On my return, Esteban brought a breakfast tray then I set off again. My legs are beginning to feel heavy: I'm no longer trekking, more strolling. I meander up to the zoo. Is this the only way of seeing toucans? I had a lovely encounter with a sloth which I had never realised were such sweet creatures. He was the two-toed variety, prettier than his extra toed cousin, with a face not unlike my border collie before I fetch his lead. He was so cute I wanted to stroke him, but thought better of it. I knew nothing of his temperament, and I could never get away with a lost finger claiming a sloth savaged me. There was also a tapir, ocelot and jaguarundi. I saw the Golden Frog for which this place is famous (only one?), and returned to town for lunch; chicken and rice and lentils and plantain, at the Funda De Bambu, where the locals eat.

Feeling well fed, I set off to find the Arboles Cuadrados, the famous square trees of the region. I eventually gave up after, I'm fairly certain, some locals sent me down a difficult trail to a river for a laugh.

"Donde son los arboles cuadrillos?"

"El camino hasta el rio, heh, heh, heh!"

However, during the course of my search I saw agoutis, humming birds, and pretty little tame finches. Well, not tame, of course, but they allowed you to get tantalisingly close. Also I came across some remarkable haciendas, which shows this is a valley for the very wealthy retired, all set in manicured parkland.

I returned, showered off the dust, took a few beers, and headed off to Ty's Bar for dinner. It is shut. It is then I realised my time in the valley had been like a monastic retreat. Dinner eventually was a tin of tuna salad and a packet of crisps. Two days later I would meet up with the Canadian couple I had chatted to whilst watching the ice hockey in Ty's, in Panama Vieja "Old Town". They couldn't stop saying how good the food was. Yeah, yeah.

On my final morning in El Valle, I strolled the lanes bordering La Cariguana before my breakfast tray, followed a humming bird around the garden, and tried some Tai Chi exercises, because this isn't the Garden of Eden, it is Shangri La. Esteban told me his grandmother's mother lived to 108! At 55 he is genuinely middle aged, though he doesn't look it. Perhaps there's something in this Tai Chi stuff after all...

Nicolas came for me in the Clio at 11:30, an hour late.

Back in Panama City

It was 75 miles from Anton back to Panama City. We had

lunch; chicken, spaghetti and rice, before touring the city. I was going to make sure Nicolas gave me a full day. At Panama Viejo which Henry Morgan ransacked in 1671, we clambered over the ruins and met up with a couple of Canadians who told me how good the food was that I had missed in Ty's bar. It is a sort of Tourist Deja Vu, where you inadvertently meet up with people sort of doing the same thing as yourself. I've seen the same Canadians at the Pyramids and the Taj Mahal. Only joking. We also spent time with an archaeologist who stopped working to explain his dig and the problems they have with a high salt water table corroding their findings. There were some beautiful religious icons preserved in these 17th century ruins, and trees full of green parrots. Nicolas was quite upset when he explained that Henry Morgan stole all the gold and silver which was normally siphoned back to Spain from here. "And for this the Queen of England, Elizabeth, made Henry Morgan Governor of Jamaica!" He sounded as indignant as if it were our present queen who had insulted Panama thus. This prompted a discussion on the value of a monarchy…with a money spinning royal wedding in the very recent past.

We set off again and on the coast road four toucans flew over the car. Finally, a tick…not seen one in a tree yet, though. Nicky took me to the vast towers being erected - mainly by Donald Trump - with apartments commanding rent of $1 million a year. Then to delightful Casco Viejo, literally the old quarter, but in reality the "new city" built in response to Morgan's destruction. Narrow paved streets with restored and restoring colourful colonial buildings, all ice creams and pastels, and at the Plaza de Francia (celebrating De Lesseps, builder of the Suez Canal, but failed engineer of the Panama Canal) a marvellous mirador; ships, islands, skyscrapers and blue ocean as a background while the real stars played in the fore. Scores of pelicans swooping and crashing into the sea, surfacing, flying off, circling and, then doing it all over again. Wonderful. And, of course, scores of happy people.

There is this atmosphere you always feel in a Latin city, as if music is playing, and there is a beat, and everyone and everything is swaying and dancing to it. And the people are smiling and laughing. And Casco Viejo was swaying and dancing and enthusing like the best of them. It was intoxicating. No to Trump towers; yes, to pelicans.

Nick then showed me the other side of the coin, some dark, brooding, gang-infested neighbourhoods before we were denied access to the Parque Municipal, which closed at 5pm. (we should have done it first?). So back to the Amador Hostal and the debate over tomorrow. I want to go to Tobago Island, but the return ferry (if on time) doesn't get in till 5:30, I have a 7:50 flight, and the trip to the airport *could* be two hours. I'd love the ferry trip and a bit of a swim, but with the assurance that the Pacific waters are too cold (the Humboldt Current which wells up from as far away as the Antarctic), I've plumped for the four-hour trek around the rainforest on the edge of the city instead.

Finally, Nick bought me a beer (with my money) at the Balboa Yacht Club. Too posh for me.

I spent my last night in Panama with Stephen Fry. There was nobody else about. But at breakfast there were a dozen or so young Americans all with their noses in bibles. I had coffee, juice and cereal, and hailed a taxi. "Metropolitan Parque" I said. "Donde?" my driver requested. I repeated it four times, slowly, and in my best Spanish accent, and showed him my walking boots. "Aah! Metropolitan Parque. I am learning English. You must speak more slowly."

I walked all five of the trails, which were scintillating. Pure rainforest in the heart of the municipality, aptly described as the lungs of the city. I had one criticism though: there was at times, a little too much traffic noise.

The stars were the leafcutter ants (I know: ubiquitous) So

many colonies, each having gouged paths for themselves to fetch their favourite vegetation to take underground for it to rot and grow fungus to feed their young. These paths must have taken years, and go up and down trees and along the forest floor for hundreds of yards. One tribe which specialised in flower petals had a trail spanning over 200 yards.

I also saw several frogs, lizards and terrapins; beautiful butterflies galore, and there was the constant buzzing from the cicadas and birdsong. Other highlights included one toucan with the biggest, bright green beak, two Geoffroy's Tamarins (mine!) and the back end of a white-nosed coati, so I don't know if it was coati, but let's say it was. A distant bird sang the most amazing lilting call, and yo ho! I saw another toucan. This one gave its call, a low croak, which I can listen out for next time. I picnicked on sardines piquante and beans out of tins, then took a taxi to the Yacht Club for a beer by the ocean. I walked back to the hostal along the Flamenco Island road, showered and settled into a hammock at the end of this magical escape: That first morning in the choking rush hour; my treks around Boquette and friendship with Daveed; my time at the Gran Kahuna on the Caribbean; the full transit of the Panama Canal; the treks in the Valley and my good friend Esteban; the old and new cities full of happy, dancing locals; the Parque Municipale.

It was a little annoying that Nick dropped me at the airport at 5 o'clock. The transfer was only 30 minutes, not the two hours he threatened. I could have gone to the island! Anyway, there I was. I cleared security and set about finding how best to dispose of the $1.80 I had cleverly left myself. I shouldn't have worried. On the main concourse were kiosks with young, heavily made-up promotion girls selling rum (with free tasting) from Panama, Costa Rica and Nicaragua. It is a wide concourse so kiosks had been set up both left and right, six in all, and I went around twice. In between I bought some Chester fries. After 12 tots of rum and some chips I was ready to board.

It is near enough 11 hours from Panama City to Amsterdam. After my evening meal with a glass of red wine I watched one movie and fell asleep. When I awoke the screen said "Time to Destination 1hr 24 minutes. The power of Caribbean Rum!

At Schiphol awaiting the short hop to Birmingham I took another health test. Losing a couple of pounds was OK, but my blood pressure was quite improved.

It occurred to me upon returning home, that I should really thank Nicolas and Natasha at GoPanama. I can't necessarily say I would recommend them, but thanks to their little inefficiencies they certainly made my adventure all that more memorable.

*

Venezuela's Lost World

A most remote waterfall is the world's highest, Angel Falls, and since nearly falling off Victoria Falls (Zambia) my quest had been to visit all the world's most important cascades. I joined an expedition to visit the southern region of Venezuela which would include climbing Roraima, the inspiration for Arthur Conan Doyle's classic The Lost World (dinosaurs marooned on a plateau and surviving into the modern era), flying around Angel Falls, navigating the Rio Akanan around the Tepuys (table top mountains) of the Gran Sabana, and many more adventures as I follow in the footsteps of that great thespian explorer, Brian Blessed (*Quest For A Lost World*, 1999). Albeit not quite so loud!

We gathered together in Caracas, the capital of Venezuela, and were led by Carlucho Perez, a proud socialist Venezuelan, complete with pony tail and a fount of knowledge. Joining us were Rod, a tall, ruddy army captain specialising in procurement; Vicky and Adam, a married couple of forensic scientists from Redditch; Lyndsay, a doctor from Guildford whose hobby was Amdram, and our local drivers Wilma and Douglas.

The adventure began, driving out of Caracas and marvelling at the hillsides covered by Favelas, South America's equivalent to shanty towns. Leaving the city behind we headed east on the Panamerican Highway, along the Atlantic coast. At the town of Barcelona we lunched on garlic mullet overlooking a lagoon which had seemingly unending flocks of cormorant migrating west. Clambering back into the minibus we turned south, eventually arriving at the country's second city, Cuidad Bolivar. Here is the only bridge (in Venezuela) that spans the mighty Orinoco river; the Angostura Bridge, reminding us that Angostura Bitters (both allegedly poisonous and restorative, the bitters are mainly used now as a cocktail flavouring) were first produced here to help the army of Simon Bolivar, that great South American freedom fighter.

Other than the impressive bridge, we also saw Jimmie Angel's Flamingo monoplane, El Rio Caroni, which is on display outside the Maracay Aviation Museum. Angel had discovered the eponymous falls when his plane crash landed on top of Auyantepui in 1937 having flown over them four years earlier. The indigenous Pemon Indian name for the falls is Kerepakupai Vena, the Waterfall of the Deepest Place.

We took in the wonderful sunset from the bridge before overnighting in a simple hotel.

Day two of our drive took us into the "wild west" as we passed gold mining shack settlements where all life appeared to revolve around the village petrol station. We had to endure many security stops where disturbingly young, armed soldiers demanded to see our yellow fever certificates and would insist on a little bribe before allowing us to drive on. In between there was a mixture of pampas and impenetrable forest. We lunched in extreme heat at a riverside bar where the owner insisted on introducing us to his pet tarantula.

Juanita was hairy, black and at least ten inches across, and this particular arachnophobe felt just a little uncomfortable holding her in the palms of his hands. We paddled in the river to cool off and were warned to beware of piranha fish. Here they are called caribes, and the mere threat of their presence brought a premature end to our paddle.

That evening we set up camp on the Gran Sabana at Kawi and our first night under canvass. Carlucho delighted in telling us over steak and Cuba libres that the giant anteater which inhabits this area could easily eviscerate you with one sweep of its massive front claws. He also showed around a photograph of himself and 20 others standing in a line holding an anaconda snake end to end. These massive constrictors prey on capybara, pig-sized guinea pigs. There are moments when gallivanting, you sit back, pinch yourself and realise how foreign the world can be.

"Are we likely to see any anteaters?" Rod asked. Carlucho smiled and shrugged enigmatically.

"What about snakes?" enquired Vicky, nervously.

"Anaconda in the Orinoco Delta, and anteaters will only turn on you if you disturb them tearing into a termite mound," assured Carlucho. "But dinosaurs on top of Roraima?" he smirked, "well there'll be Geoff…"

Thanks!

After breaking camp, we engaged in one last moment of luxury; bathing and playing in the forest waterfall; climbing up and sliding down the slippery rocks with a sploosh into warm, fresh water, in the middle of a forest with dappled sunshine and the singing and squawking of birds all around; great fun. But now was the time to begin the trek to Roraima. This is the largest of all the 115 tepuys which dominate the Canaima National Park in the Guiana Highlands. Tepuys (Pemon Indian for Homes of the Gods) are straight sided, table top sandstone mountains and are considered to be among the world's oldest geological formations. At over 9,000 feet, with sheer sides and over 20 square miles of summit, no wonder Conan Doyle imagined Roraima could contain a prehistoric "Lost World".

We had three days of progressively more difficult terrain, but after collecting our porters and supplies we almost immediately picnicked in a forest glade, it was lunchtime after all, which we shared with butterflies and poison arrow frogs. Then it was off onto the treeless plain which constituted the first approach. We could see the cloud covered tepuys in the distance, it was such a huge terrain and sky that we could also see and anticipate the heavy squalls of rain which found us covered in plastic ponchos.

After five slogging hours of dodging showers and marvelling at the scenery we arrived at the first camp, bedraggled, drenched (in spite of the ponchos), but only slightly dispirited. It is a wooden hut where we cook and eat, overlooking the swollen river Tek. We sleep outside in tents erected on the rock. Even though boots and clothing were soaked, we had managed to follow the golden rule; "Keep your bedding dry". The porters had set up camp and cooked us a beef dinner. A few warm beers led me to my second night under canvas, which I still find hugely uncomfortable. Lying awake under circumstances like these I am liable to night najjers where I imagine all sorts of weird experiences. Tonight's nightmare included trying to avoid the swinging claws of anteaters whilst being trampled on by huge tarantulas and shrinking from the venom-dripping jaws of a giant snake.

Our camp had one luxury. Out of your tent and a five-minute walk uphill led you to a wooden hut with no door, but a toilet. Fellow adventurers will understand when I say that long-drop toilets can be a rare comfort. As you cling on to the ropes to avoid falling in, the view over the river to the mountains was magnificent. It was to be our last sit down for a week.

The next day began with the ford of the river. Fast flowing and over knee deep the priority is to keep your backpack, and hence your bedding dry. Any sort of footwear creates too much drag, and I have found that the best way to create purchase for your feet and to feel for and find the best footholds is to paddle in your socks. I toppled over once but only suffered a wet bottom.

There was another ford to face in the next valley, but this was successfully negotiated before we engaged on a strenuous six-hour uphill trek to base camp. We fell into camp exhausted and could only gaze directly upwards in wonder at the sheer face of the mountain. How can there be a path, we thought? It looked impossible. We dined on pasta and after a brief reconnaissance of the early slopes, took an early night. This third night under canvas was better and we were woken at six for a pancake breakfast. Over breakfast I was proud to be chosen as the pathfinder to lead the assault on the summit. It is probably due to my experience, I thought. But, "We didn't want to have to keep stopping for you to catch up", was the explanation Carlucho gave with a knowing grin.

Only feeling slightly deflated, I led the party up those same slopes we had visited the night before and which had lulled us into a false sense of security as we had hopefully envisaged a gentle zigzag up the face. There were two hours of joyful scrambling before we actually hit the wall, and some serious hard work. We encountered an increasingly tighter switchback of treacherously wet pathways. The fairy glades of trees and shrubs from which hung or clung all manner of ferns, lichen and mosses soon gave way to unstable, dangerous scree. There were some wonderful views across the Gran Sabana below us, but too many loose boulders for us to lose concentration for a second. Should you dislodge one there would be the warning shout of "Below!", and those people behind put their heads closer to the wall and know not to look up. There were also chasms to negotiate and some wonderfully weird, pendulous waterfalls to trek through. Water falling in sheets from the summit waving to and fro as if the gods were swinging a hosepipe from above.

At midday we reached the Lost World and clasped hands. Exhausted, I flung off my backpack, lay down on a flat slab and immediately fell asleep bathed in the sunshine. The respite was brief as Carlucho insisted on taking us to the highest point of the tepuy where we took lunch before tramping off to find our cave.

There was the eeriest feel about the plateau. It was silent as a cathedral with astonishingly eroded sandstone statuary all around. Among the sculptures were little pools of green oases where only the hardiest flora could cling to life.

After setting up camp in our cave and resting awhile I strolled to the edge of the Lost World, this island in the sky, and sat down with my legs dangling over the precipice and surveyed the rest of the world. Below me and stretching far into the distance, the unending Gran Sabana looking like a lumpy baize cloth. In the distance, clouds at my height and emanating from them the occasional flash of lightning dashing down to earth. I sat and stared till long after sunset, by which time the fireflies had joined me.

I contemplated the dusk. Wherever you are in the world, and dusk falls, lights begin to appear; street lamps, house and office lights, cars and so on. Well here, on top of Roraima, looking out over thousands of square miles of savannah and forest, there wasn't one single light; twinkling or otherwise. Just me and the fireflies.

Then the stars come out. I believe the first one accompanying the sunset would be the planet Venus. But as the sky grows blacker you can make out the constellations; the Plough and Orion's belt, Cassiopeia and Cygnus the swan and the Seven Sisters, and then you begin to see the Milky Way reminding me I am on the same continent as the Incas who looked into the centre of our Galaxy mirrored in the Urubamba river valley and called it Sacred. There are plenty of twinkling lights now, in this window into infinity.

Back at camp, our Indian porters have once again excelled in producing an admirable meal of beef stew. They sit cross legged and with a white plastic cutting board perched on their knees and prepare all of the vegetables and meat expertly. We wolf it down and are in our sleeping bags fully clothed by eight o'clock. It is cool up here.

Early to bed means early rising, and we are up and ready for exploring the plateau before the sun is fully up. We hiked up and down and through chasms, crevasses and craters, across streams and beaches strewn with crystals. Always the sculptured formations black with lichen, but when the light strikes them, pink, white and green producing hallucinatory descriptions; a horse, lizard, turtle, ape, rocket ship, tortoise, frog, two kissing dinosaurs, and much more. We even saw a real coati.

We took lunch at a sinkhole called La Fosa, and trekked to the triple point where the borders of Brazil, Venezuela and Guyana meet. At one stage there was a very depressing episode. We heard the beating of a helicopter's rotors so hid among the rocks as it landed. A couple emerged from the cockpit, walked around for a few minutes then got back in and it flew away. It would have been no more surreal if we had witnessed an alien landing.

The next day we woke to rain and cold mist, but we were on a schedule, so broke camp and headed across the Roraima plateau for the descent. Today we are attempting a double down descent to the river Tek, attempting to go down in one day what it took two days to climb.

First there was the wall, very steep and heart stopping, through the waterfalls, up and down until we reach the forest with slippery clay, and roots, branches and trunks to swing or clamber from, or trip over! With aching knees and screaming thighs, we reach base camp and lunch. It is no wonder we are tired after 5 days of hard trekking. On the way down I lost count of the times I looked around and said "I can't believe we climbed that!". We continued our descent across difficult rocky terrain where it is so easy to lose your footing, to the two rivers. We crossed the one then stripped off and played in the next. Glorious fun sliding in and out of the rapids, and so therapeutic for our aching bodies. A final, sixth night under canvas, and it doesn't get any easier.

Our final day hiking on the Gran Sabana is under blue skies and we have the twin tepui of Kukenan and Roraima behind us. So often on our approach they were hidden under skirts of cloud, today we have them in full view. The trek is slow and cumbersome, and towards the end Carlucho goes missing. Then suddenly he arrives in a truck with crates of ice cold beer and, weirdly, pineapples and papaya. We feasted and drank copiously and said goodbye to our Indian porters (who now, Carlucho assured us, would take our tips and "piss them up against the wall"). Clambering aboard the cruiser someone puts Queen's A Night At The Opera on full blast and we sang full throated until we reached our hotel at the border town of St Elena de Uairen and a bed!

Today a new adventure starts and we awoke, well rested and rather overhung to the most amazing dawn chorus of hoots and screeches, twitterings and crowing. After breakfast we were taken to a small airstrip and bundled into a Cessna. The pilot, a middle aged tall distinguished looking man with silver hair and a huge moustache climbs in to join us, straps himself in, throws a few switches and the engine bursts into life. He has with him a rather imposing looking black leather briefcase, and he solemnly opens it to retrieve, one would imagine the flight plan and passenger manifest. Instead he simply lifts out his sandwich box and partakes of a late breakfast.

We take off and are immediately above the Gran Sabana and can see the array of flat top mountains in the distance. We fly low over forest and lakes and rivers which snake below us and catch the sun which blinds us in momentary flashes. We gain height as we are heading specifically to the Auyantepui, off which flows the Angel Falls into the Devil's Canyon, and the pilot circles the tepui and inside points out the little sliver of water which at three times the height of the Eiffel Tower makes up the world's highest, tallest waterfall. To be honest it is merely a small stream of water falling off a mountain which happens to have a steep side for 3,212 feet. We'll see the bottom, where it lands in a few days, and get a better idea of its magnificence.

No sooner had we landed at the village of Kamarata and said goodbye to Ramon, that an Indian in full headdress takes us in tow. He introduces himself as Billy and explains how tree frogs are used to create the poison for his tribe's blowpipe arrows. He then leads us on a hike up a canyon with a fast flowing stream to a sinkhole where we swim and play under a huge waterfall. It feels much better to be in one than just looking down at one from a great height in a tiny, cramped aeroplane with scratched and grimy windows.

Finally, in a day of so many contrasts, Billy walks us down a slipway into the waters of the Rio Akanan where a dug out is waiting to take us the three-day journey to Canaima. The river is low and we have to portage to lift the boat away from the rocks on four occasions, regularly falling into the rapids. It is slow progress and the last hour to camp has to be undertaken in total darkness. We made a human chain to take luggage and supplies into camp where we enjoyed a chicken dinner and one of the most comfortable night's sleep I have ever had; in a woollen hammock. The hammock is all encompassing, and encourages your body into a foetal position from where you sleep literally cocooned.

The campsite is very simple. A tarpaulin is swung across trees in case it rains. We are in a rainforest, after all, and it does do what it says on the tin! The hammocks are similarly attached to the trees. There is a small seating area where food is cooked and eaten, and about 40 yards away a sit down toilet which flushes with buckets of water filled from the river. You wash and clean teeth in the river. On this first night we saw a gecko, only about 4 inches long, but it had caught a cockroach almost as big as itself, and the insect was half eaten, but the front half which wasn't eaten was projecting from the gecko's mouth and still struggling as the gecko chewed slowly and methodically. We watched for over two hours this monumental struggle. By the morning both creatures had vanished and we reckoned the gecko had eventually managed to consume the whole roach, or maybe a snake had come along and consumed both.

The next day is one of meandering down the loops of the river, constantly in the shadow of Ayantepui. One moment it will be on our left, the next straight ahead, then to our right, then behind us. The dugout is less than comfortable and I take to sitting on my thin foam mattress as the going appears slow and laboured. You find yourself joyfully anticipating the next rapids so we can get out and walk!

There is a remarkable lack of wildlife. Had there been birds we wouldn't hear them above the outboard motor, but we see none, only the black water, green overhanging canopy, occasional sky, and the ever looming mountain.

We found a beach for lunch, and Carlucho asked us to wait whilst the lightened boat could negotiate a particularly difficult portage. So we ate and swam and snoozed and watched whilst the dugout got completely stuck. "We'll have to go and help" I told Rod and Adam, so the youngsters swam from above the rapids in a long arc in which the current could easily have taken them onto treacherous rocks, and I chose the below the rapids route. By the time I had to turn to swim upstream to the boat, I was already exhausted and eventually I had to be hauled into the dugout like a wet fish. Rod and Adam arrived about the same time. After we had recovered it was all hands to work in a concerted effort to edge the boat forward and rock it off the rocks and into deeper water. Twice Carlucho and Rod fell and were nearly sucked under the boat, their heads could easily have been trapped between rushing water, rock and wooden gunwhale. Loosening the boat then could have been fatal!

Inch by inch, we gradually dislodged the heavy boat until eventually we could put extra weight (me) into the bow for it to tip into the deeper water. That was a bit too hairy! We meandered a few more hours before landing at a pleasant clearing and preparing chicken with rice, pineapple and banana for dinner. Following a few beers Lindsay and I tried to sing the whole of Madame Butterfly. Her Cho Cho San was really good, my Pinkerton less so, as was my Suzuki. Our caterwauling probably guaranteed the wildlife gave our camp a wide berth. Apart, that is for a huge green spider which I found clambering across my chest. Deep joy!

Our final day on the river began with a swim and a pancake breakfast and the exciting news that today we would see the foot of Angel Falls. We set off downstream, then turned left into the Churum river and had to battle several sets of rapids, like salmon leaping upstream. Eventually we concede that with the river so low, we couldn't make it to Devil's Canyon and had to content ourselves with a beach and lagoon surrounded by the forest at the foot of Auyantepui. To come so far and not see where the falls land was so frustrating but we were reassured by Carlucho. "Honestly" he said with a shrug, "the water has so far to fall that by the time it reaches the bottom it has evaporated. All there is to see is a pile of rocks!"

We set off back downstream and the heavens opened to make for a really uncomfortable journey. To the bemusement of Carlucho and the crew we struck up West Side Story. My "Something's Coming", and Lindsay's "I Feel Pretty" helped the time fly by, and when Rod and the scientists joined in with "America", we had the boat really rocking. I explained to Carlucho that we Brits know how to deal with a rainy day.

The following day the sun came back out and we had a scorching two-hour trek over savannah to reach Canaima. In the middle of the wilderness we came across a gleaming silver

Dakota which had crashed here many years before. Stripped of everything useful, the empty aluminium fuselage of the plane was left as a reminder that out here in the middle of nowhere, 20th century (or even 21st) technology is just so much rusting scrap.

In the village, we passed a school where children were chanting their times tables and came to a tree under which lay dead and dying cicadas next to a whitewashed wall. These huge crickets, as big as a starling in flight, are so attracted to the shiny wall that they fly and crash straight into it. And you think moths around flames were stupid.

In the afternoon, as the others slept, Carlucho took me to a lake which had several waterfalls flowing into it. We swam from sandbank to sandbank until we reached one of the cataracts. "This is so picture skew," said Carlucho, and I was a little confused by his English until I realised he was trying to say a word which previously he had only seen in print. As I was trying to explain picturesque to him, it suddenly dawned on me where I had seen this array of three waterfalls before. It was the "Murial" (sic) which had adorned Hilda Ogden's wall for so many years in Coronation Street! The things you come half way across the world to find!

Later we flew back to Caracas and were joined by Gloria, Carlucho's girlfriend, a beautiful Latin woman who reminded me of Clive James's resident musician and comedienne, Margarita Pracatan. Together we drove out to Chichirivichi, which is billed as a luxury Caribbean beach resort, but in truth is a poor shanty fishing village with a dirty beach. The hotel was pleasant enough, and the red snapper dinner was a delight. From the balcony I could see humming birds and delighted at the sight of a three-foot iguana climbing a palm tree right next to me.

There was one final adventure and the chance to try out an urban myth. I borrowed a snorkel, mask and fins and headed for the beach in order to swim out to the coral reef. The reef was mostly dead, but there was some colour and the usual tropical fish; parrots and wrasses, grunts and butterflies and a spectacular fierce looking but mostly harmless moray eel. Whilst lazily traversing the rocks, the usually clear, warm water suddenly became clouded and fuzzy and I felt a million pinpricks on my skin, nothing serious or that painful, just like pins and needles. I realised I had swum through a bloom of tiny jellyfish.

Back at the hotel I filled a coke bottle with (my own) urine and showered in it. I can assuredly declare that this apparently weird cure for jellyfish stings does work. The all over tingling sensation totally disappeared and I was able to take a more conventional shower and shampoo and join my fellow explorers for a final dinner.

So, "Where next?" was the predictable question, over drinks as the sun set into the Caribbean Sea.

"I've tasked myself to see the world's greatest waterfalls, so it has to be Niagara" I said with little conviction. I had no real ambition to visit the brash and touristy American/Canadian attraction.

"No!" Carlucho insisted. "You must see what is truly the world's greatest array of waterfalls at Iguazu" he announced proudly clutching Gloria closer, and she was grinning and nodding approvingly.

Where?" everyone said.

*

Las Vegas Through Dad's Eyes & Fantasy Fest

I've never been a gambler. Well, I used to have an annual flutter on the Grand National, everyone does, but I have only ever once returned to collect winnings, and that was the year of the false start. I did also dabble with casinos in my twenties, after chucking out time from night clubs. As one of the last big spenders, I would go to a roulette table, buy a fiver's worth of chips and put them on 8,11 or 29,32 splits, then marvel at the antics of more devoted gamblers as they spread chips like butter all over the table. My numbers would occasionally come up and I would indulge in a little spreading of my own, but generally I found that the despair of losing always outweighed the joy of winning.

So, not being a gambler, you might question why I would choose to visit Las Vegas.

Two reasons: on the one hand, the observer can appreciate the bigger picture far better than an active participant, without the pain; on the other, this remarkable city built into the desert has far more to offer than the roll of a dice, spin of a wheel, or clunking churn of slot machines being fed relentlessly by obese automatons.

Las Vegas is the gateway to the Grand Canyon, Monument Valley, Route 66, and much, much more. My main motivation, however, was the realisation of one of my father's dreams. He had passed away in the Spring, and never fulfilled his ambition to see where Tony Bennet and Frank Sinatra sang, or experience the wild west of Johns Ford and Wayne. My adventure to Nevada, Arizona and Utah that 'fall' was in his memory.

I left Heathrow at noon and arrived via a steamy Houston at the Days Inn on Kovak, just behind the L.V. Strip. It's breakfast time to me, but at 2:20 am Pacific Time Zone, the night has just begun. This is a 24-hour city.

I dropped my bags and left in a hurry to explore (something I'd once done upon arrival in Athens; after two hours of sightseeing I decided to return to the hotel, but where was it, what was the street name, and worse, what was the hotel name? That little adventure took another two hours of searching before locating the vague memory of the hotel's whereabouts).

It is 30 degrees in the middle of the night, but as light as day as I emerge onto the bustling Strip. Opposite the Eiffel Tower I discover the beautiful Italianate structure that is the Bellagio Hotel. Escalators take you up to the bridge across the Strip, (stretch limos dominate the traffic below) and down the other side. The towering hotel is lit up elegantly in blue and white, but its eight-acre lake and fountains steal the show. I skirted around the lake to enter. The huge lobby was an ocean of floral display, both actual and Murano glass. My visual and olfactory senses were thrust into overdrive. Then there are miles of marble and carpeted halls and gaming floors. It is a mosque, a Mecca to Roulette, Poker, Black Jack and Craps. Yet it all seems so clean and civilised despite intelligent people throwing their money down the drain. There is neither cigarette nub nor gum stain to be found anywhere. The staff, so polite and friendly, each an Adonis or Aphrodite, seek only to serve refreshments, all complimentary, and ask that you play the tables or feed the slots. I didn't, I just wanted to explore, but had to pretend to be tired and go to bed to adjust to the time difference. I reluctantly returned to the modest Days Inn.

I breakfasted at eight on a stack of pancakes and bacon with maple syrup, and paid the $8 bill with a ten (must leave a tip, I thought, we're in the USA). On my way back to the room, a young waitress calls to me across the pool, "Sir, sir!" she cries out. I suppose I'd not left enough tip, so reluctantly I returned. "Sir, you left a fifty-dollar bill", she said breathlessly. "I guess the money is still confusing for you" and she pressed $42 into my hand. I stood open mouthed as she smiled and said "Y'all have a nice day now" and she turned and went back to the restaurant.

I spent the morning in and out of hotels; Mandalay Bay, Luxor, Excalibur and Venetian. I discovered the gaming floors are all virtually identical, and everything else plastic. The Eiffel Tower, the Pyramids, Rome, New York, a Venetian canal complete with Gondola, all plastic. There's nothing pretentious here. You get what you expect and nothing more. This place is quite happy to be simply a scaled-down plastic artifice.

It is Sunday, so at 11am I found myself seated at the Bellagio Lake with about 2,000 others, ready for the first performance. A haunting melody began to play across the water, instantly recognisable as the penny whistle from Celine Dion's 'My Heart Will Go On'. In the centre of the eight-acre lake, the fountains are in a line and they begin to flow into the air and wave and oscillate in time to the music. "Near, far, wherever you are..." They blast upwards at crescendo like a thunderclap and are synchronised with a light show. At the key change, the huge surge sounded like a whip crack, and then they relaxed, and for the next half hour everyone's senses were assaulted gloriously with more specially selected power ballads. I was tired and emotional from such a long journey, and admit I had to weep with joy. The whole choreographed effect is so typically big and brash, but it does leave you drained with delight.

After a Mexican lunch I slept by the Day's Inn pool and ventured out early evening for the shows at Caesar's Palace, Treasure Island and The Mirage (a volcano, all plastic). I loved the gardens and water features of the Flamingo, but always crept back to the Bellagio. On my final visit of a packed day there was Henry Mancini's theme from Pink Panther, Shirley Bassey's 'Big Spender' and Elton John's 'Your Song'. Somewhat twee and audacious, yes, but how could you not fall in love with this unashamedly hedonistic playground.

The next morning, I left the Day's Motel and joined a small group tour led by an amiable French-Canadian, Michel. There were ten of us crammed into some sort of Chevrolet Land cruiser. He drove us first to the massive Hoover Dam, built during the Depression to harvest power and irrigation from the Colorado River, it created Lake Mead, the largest man-made reservoir in the US, which provides for Nevada, Arizona and California.

Crossing the dam, we entered Arizona, a new time zone, and the Mojave Desert. At Kingman we followed Route 66 to Seligman and onto Williams. At a height of 6000 feet, there was a welcome crisp coolness to the evening. We made several stops on the famous Route 66, the Mother Road, America's Main Street, but just like Bates' Motel, the highway by-pass had left it dead and unused. "Only tourists come here now," said Michel as we left one shop, the tumble weed rolling where the wind had whipped up the sand to cover any kerbs separating the sidewalk. A train hooter echoed hauntingly across the desert, reminding us of so many American films. Everyone, I'm told, loves the sound of a train in the distance.

At Williams, the gateway to the Grand Canyon NP we visited Pete's Route 66 Gas Station Museum and drank beer. It seemed only fitting.

That evening Michel booked the group into a simple hotel with a simple bar, dance hall and Country and Western duo; really bare surroundings. At home we'd call it a "spit 'n' sawdust pub", however, they did a great steak and cheap beer, leaving everyone happy, if not exactly singing along with the C & W caterwauling. I chatted with Michel. Something must have gone wrong with his career at some stage, he was well past retirement age. Still, I suppose he loved what he did.

"I moved to ze states over 40 years ago," he said in an unmistakeable French accent. "Couldn't wait to leave Canada. It wasn't just ze never ending winters, but ze folks, zey have so many chips on zer shoulders. Zey hate ze Frenchies, who hate zem right back. Zen zere are ze "lazy immigrants", and worst of all ze "free-loading natives" (Michel did that speech marks sign like rabbit's ears) Give zem a beer and zey become loud and obnoxious. Still, zey love your Queen."

I'd experienced Canadians in the Caribbean during what they call Spring Break (Whitsuntide), and Michel was not wrong, especially about the beer!

I woke early, and breakfasted with the group. We were beginning to get to know each other. There was Nick and Phil, two Grenadier Guardsmen on leave. Both over 6 feet 4 inches, wherever we stopped they just ran and ran, always choosing the most arduous uphill track. By the end of the trip they were asking for the children's menu in the restaurants, so huge were the portions. Tim and Chrissy were clingy honeymooners, loathe to let each other out of their sight. Val and Lucy were two singleton forty-somethings, travelling together for safety as well as company. They were accountants, commuters to the City. And Mary and Steve, a couple of retired Scots. Mary had mobility problems and the pair never ventured far from any stopping point.

Today was Grand Canyon day. It is not often in your life you can prepare yourself for one of those life affirming occasions.

After wolfing down pancakes with maple syrup and bacon, we drove for two hours to the Papillon Grand Canyon Helicopter port. There was no indication on the drive we were about to see one of the world's greatest iconic landscapes. We just drove through even desert brush, pretty mundane really.

At the heliport we were split into two groups, Michel didn't fly, and Steve and Mary didn't fancy the flight, fitted with earphones for the pilot's commentary and given a short safety briefing before climbing into the two 4 seater (behind pilot and co-pilot) craft. My first helicopter ride anywhere. The engines started and the rotors began their gyration. Once the noise had hit ear-splitting capacity, the vehicle gently lifted into the air, slightly tipped forward and sped off. It was just more of the same, desert scrub, but going by faster, when suddenly, bang, we were over the edge and into the vast void of the Canyon itself. It was certainly a breath-taking moment as the ground fell away from beneath us and we were almost instantly suspended a mile above the most sublimely, blindingly, indescribable landscape. Every colour of green was the flora that descended into and covered the floor of the canyon; every shade of shining red and brown was the earth and rocks and shadows cast by the formations which rose up spectacularly inside the canyon.

The Grand Canyon is four to 18 miles wide, over a mile deep, and 277 miles long. It has been home to Native Americans for thousands of years, was first seen by Europeans in 1570, and has been a protected area since the presidency of Theodore Roosevelt. Since the Colorado River started cutting the gorge six million years ago it has exposed nearly two billion years of geological history.

As the helicopter descended and ascended to pick out named formations, we occasionally had a glimpse of the Colorado River as it snaked beneath us. It is amazing to believe that this tiny sliver of water has alone created this vast fortress of beauty, slowly carving out and eroding the gorge and leaving behind numerous rock strata as the Colorado Plateau rose around it. The canyon walls indicate the geological ages with different coloured levels of varying thicknesses, attesting to the laying down of a variety of lime and sand stones as ancient seas waxed and waned, and deserts rose and fell over the aeons of its development. There has also been volcanic activity and the evidence of Ice Age melts which caused a widening of the river. In modern geological times the type of erosion which has moulded the marvellously misshapen mesas and buttes has been simple weathering.

All too soon we are back at the heliport and I am anxious to don my walking boots and see as much of the canyon as possible. Michel drops us at Mather Point, and after spending time breathing in the views down into the canyon with its sculptured domes and pyramids, and attempting to click the enormous panorama, I begin my trek. I'm on the Southern Rim and I follow the Hermit's Road West. The route is constantly punctuated by detours, overlooks and viewing points. Down below is the Phantom Ranch, from Yavapoi Observation Station there are 180 degree views of Havasupai to the West and Desert View to the East. Then there was Yaki Point on the Kaibab Trail, leading to Grandview Point from where I could see buttes named after shrines and temples. There was even the unmistakable sheen of the Colorado River itself. Then there was Maricopa, Powell, Hopi, Mojave, The Abyss and Monument Creek. I ended up after about ten miles and six hours of hiking at Hermit's Rest. If only I'd had the strength to hike back, but I took the easy way out and returned via the shuttlebus just in time for the sunset. In those last few hours as the sun sinks and creates longer shadows, the colours and hues of the Grand Canyon shift constantly. You can never have enough of this: the grandest of grand vistas.

The Grand Canyon is not a suicide hotspot, unlike our own Beachy Head, but there are around 50 falls a year from the rim, of which two or three are fatal. The biggest danger appears to be people feigning falling then re-appearing for that "Ta-Da" moment of humorous relief. Another problem in recent times has come from the fashion for taking selfies. Narcissists and lovers of the selfie-stick beware: the most spectacular picture could also be your last.

That night was spent in the unimaginatively named 'Grand Canyon Inn and Motel' located in the similarly prosaic Grand Canyon Village. Typical tourist rip-off destination foisted upon a captive market, but I spent the morning sitting by the watchtower at Desert View marvelling as the early morning haze created a bluish tinge to the canyon walls, buttes and mesas. Beyond is the desert and this is the Navajo reservation; a huge, barren corner of Arizona, Utah and Colorado which has been "allowed" to the Navajo, and out of which they are making a Nation.

We drove to The Navajo Monument then hiked down into the Tsegi Canyon to visit the cliff dwellings of Kits'iil. Strategically built by the Anasazi people of mud brick under the overhang of the cliff, the buildings and artefacts remain well preserved which adds to the mystery of why the village was completely abandoned in about 1300 AD, less than 50 years since its first occupation. Some believe a great drought caused the migration, while Hopi legend has it that children of the Snake Clan bit their neighbours to death.

We lunched at Kayenta and moved on to Monument Valley. Everybody knows this place because of the director John Ford and his star cowboy John Wayne who have used the scenery as a backdrop to so many iconic Westerns; Stagecoach, She Wore a Yellow Ribbon, and The Searchers to name but a few. From the Monument Valley Visitor Centre, an old trading post, is the most amazing view. The dark orange desert vanishes into the distance left, right, and ahead, leaving a huge sky and giant deep red buttes. These are precipitous sided monoliths rising straight up from the desert floor. Two of the most famous stand in front of you. They are the Mittens; flat topped like fingerless gloves with a sole thumb jutting up from their sides, 700 feet high. The times the US Cavalry have ridden between them.

Here we picked up our Navajo guide. A tall sturdy man with noble features and a quiet, serious demeanour, not unlike Chief Bromden, the narrator and major protagonist of One Flew Over the Cuckoo's Nest. Dave took us on a magical two-and-a-half-hour safari into the valley to marvel and wonder at the shapes and sizes of the buttes and mesas, to describe how weathering (ice, water and wind) had created such features, and try to explain some of the mysterious wall carvings. We saw Tear Drop Arch, the Sun's Eye, Ear of the Wind, and the Eagle Cave. At the latter Dave asked us to lie on our backs, and above we could see the Eagle's head with feathers and a single round eye which revealed the sky. He told us to close our eyes and think the sweetest of thoughts. Then he serenaded us with the most hauntingly beautiful flute. I thought of dad, and wept. It was the most moving of moments.

On our return, Dave tells us of Kokopelli, the Navajo spirit of the seasons, on his whim decided the harvests, therefore wealth or hardship. Elsewhere the flute playing, headdress wearing, mischievous dancing figure represents both fertility and agriculture and has become the god of tourist trinkets.

Bidding farewell to Dave, we drove to Mexican Hat, a small town named for the mesa that resembles a sombrero that stands just north of the San Juan river crossing. A pleasant overnight stop where we drank cold beer and watched bats flying along the river while the moths they were chasing massed around the electric bulbs.

Just outside Mexican Hat, the San Juan river flows into a series of tight turns forming Gooseneck Canyon, a real Kodak moment. This is a perfect example of an incised meander, where the water course has cut sharply into the bedrock creating symmetrical sides to a deep canyon, in this case forming a perfect tear drop, or gooseneck. From here we drove across the desert and climbed the far mesa which overlooked the Valley of the Gods. We arrived at Halls Crossing and took the ferry across Lake Powell (the second largest man-made reservoir in the US which is currently, due to drought and level of water usage slightly larger than Lake Mead) to Bullfrog. There is little or no vegetation on the banks of the lake leaving a sense of lifelessness. The blue sky, the brown rock, the blue still water, simple discoloured bleaching of the shoreline indicating different water levels. We are now in Utah, Mormon country. From Bullfrog we drove on the dirt track Burr Trail to Boulder for Lunch. Quite a morning for sightseeing; a geologist's dream with layers and erosion and shapes and formations and colours and harsh, hardy vegetation.

Risking sightseeing overload, Michel drives us to Bryce Canyon, part of Bryce National Park. We pass through and by the Grand Staircase-Escalante National Monument, Capitol Reef NP, the Water Pocket Fold divide, and the Henry Mountains. This is also a Palaeontologist's dream; dinosaur fossils dating over 80 million years old have been found here, including that of a tyrannosaur which pre-dates our old friend T. Rex by some 13 million years.

At Bryce Point we walked the rim passed Inspiration Point, through Fairyland Point and on to Sunset Point. Overlooking the canyon all the way (about five miles), the extent of the views is awe inspiring with incredible rock formations. There are stupas and fissures and grottos and all forms of coloured outcrops, the colours attributable to the different mineral deposits. The most amazing and mysterious being what appear to be giant stalagmites rising from the canyon floor. Red, orange and white, there is a magical symmetry to these Hoodoos which look like soldiers at attention, and are also known as Sentinels. Hoodoos are soft rock eroded out of softer rock, but topped by harder rock fortified by magnesium. This dolomite protects the hoodoo from further erosion even though the hoodoos of Bryce overcome over 200 ice/thaw cycles a year.

At the Bryce Canyon Inn we are allowed only beer with our burger meals, such is the Mormon way. We meet Madelyn, our waitress, who at only 18 is married with five children. She is a charming young mother who can see nothing unusual in having already had five pregnancies.
In the morning I walked the Navajo Loop, down among the sentinels themselves, gradually rising to Sunset Point. At one moment a gorgeous mountain bluebird alighted on the sparse branch of a bristlecone pine no more than five feet away and warbled a lovely serenade.

Michel, or "Mikey" as he is now known, drove the group to the highest point of Bryce Canyon, Rainbow Point, at over 9,000 feet, then we drove north to Zion NP for lunch and walks. What a pity we had done Bryce first, because while Zion is excellent, everything is just smaller and seemingly less significant than what we had previously experienced. I made three hikes, the best of which was to the Weeping Rock, where a hanging garden of lush greenery dangles from the overhang, watered from Echo Canyon above.

We spent the evening in Springdale. It doesn't take long to understand that Utah is very much a state of simple, homely, wooden dwellings with porch swinging activity being about as strenuous as it gets. Tomorrow it is back to brash, 21st century Nevada; all bright lights, gambling and golf courses. Probably befitting our current location, our meal was simply pizza and beer. We met an elderly couple, Elspeth and Abe, and approached the topic every member of the Church of Latter Day Saints dreads; What do you think of the material success of the Osmonds?

It turns out that the Mormon nation are very proud of their most illustrious of ambassadors, not least for the amount of excellent PR the brothers and sister have provided for nearly five decades. They love Donny and Jimmy, but are a little sad for Marie who has had mixed fortunes in love, and found tragedy when her son, Michael, one of eight children committed suicide at 18. A daughter, Jessica on coming out, gave yet another opportunity for the church to embrace modern society.

Abe recounted the story of the Californian seagull, which is the state bird of Utah. In 1948, the new settlers of Salt Lake City faced starvation when a plague of locusts (crickets) descended on the town and began to devour their second harvest. Like a biblical miracle, legions of seagulls suddenly arrived from the ocean, over 500 miles away, descended on the swarm and ate them, thus saving some 4,000 Mormon pioneers. The story is true, though it is now known that the birds were native to the local Great Salt Lake. Why let a little local knowledge get in the way of a miracle; and it made for a wonderful pulpit parable to prove God was on their side.

After a morning spent hiking up to the three Emerald Pools of Zion, we left Utah following the Virgin River then descending the Veterans Memorial Hill which seemed to follow the Virgin River gorge forever, down and down and down, until we finally levelled out into the Mojave Desert and the town of Mesquite where the water from the lawn sprinklers evaporates before it hits the ground. Mikey stops at the plush Oasis Hotel and we leave the air conditioned people carrier to hit a wall of heat. Not for long though, in seconds we are in the cool reception of the casino where it is all about to hit the fan.

The casino had put on a lovely buffet for the princely sum of $3, and included souvenirs; craps dice and playing cards to take with us. "Zey just would like you to spend some time here playing ze tables and ze slots," explained Mikey.

OK, I thought, if I must, I'll have a dabble. I'm not a fan of Blackjack; too slow and regimented, and I can't be bothered to try to read the cards (takes too long to find a pattern anyway).

And I don't like the way American Roulette has the extra Double Zero which increases the odds on winning. So I resolved just to have a little play on the slots. Be back on the bus in ten minutes.

As the last of the big spenders I obtained $5 worth of quarters and proceeded to feed the nearest machine. It was the usual, lights flashing everywhere, with completely indecipherable instructions about bonus nudge options and whatever. So, after a couple of spins the four windows go cherry, melon, bar and, I don't know, banana, or something, nothing to indicate any sort of winning line, and the machine starts going "Kerchung, Kerchung, Kerchung...", and it is throwing out quarters, and won't stop. Someone passes me a paper cup, and I fill that one, then I fill another, and eventually, after having attracted quite a crowd, the machine stops. I feel slightly embarrassed to have two pockets bulging with coins, and two large coffee cups full to the brim. I take what I assume are my ill-gotten gains to the change window and the non-plussed attendant hands me back $215!

Back on the land cruiser we shared our experiences. Three of us had won over two hundred dollars in a similarly unpredictable, haphazard way.

Now here's the thing about Nevada. It's not just Vegas, but wherever you go there are slots. The hardware store, the grocery, the mail office, the bar (slots slotted into the counter), the public toilets, the airport concourse, everywhere. And now I am hooked. Wherever I find myself, I craftily invest a handful of quarters. And that's how it gets you.

I have one more night in Las Vegas before flying to Miami tomorrow for Fantasy Fest. So, first we have another Vegas night out. Michel takes us to the Fremont Street Experience, a trip into the old down town area. This could have buckled under due to the success of the upmarket hotels at the other end of the strip, but a fantastic laser light show has been created featuring Star Wars type adventure scenarios just above your head, keeping the neck muscles strained and the tourists coming and the shops and bars open.

Mikey bids his farewell at this point, the soldiers and accountants have gone, and Steve and Mary are resting in the hotel. That just leaves me and the honeymooners. They'd not seen the Bellagio!

If I can do no more with my life, then it is complete as I introduce Tim and Chrissy, the star-crossed lovers, to the most romantic place they will ever see in their lives. We walked up through the strip, passing incredibly shining edifices left and right, icons to the gods of gambling and hedonism. My mind drifts to another place and another time, not so far away and not so long ago where the icons are sculpted mesas and buttes, the people are the Navajo nation, and the god is Kokopelli, he who spreads mischief and devilry. Then the fountains cracked into life, the music floated over the lake, and the ballet began.

24 hours later and I am in the sunshine state of Florida. It is only a stopover though as I have been recommended to see the famous Fantasy Fest of Key West. From Miami airport I had taken a Greyhound to the Keys. The Keys are a series of islands off the southern tip of Florida all connected by bridges and freeways and culminating in Key West, a beautifully maintained old town which is also the southernmost point of the USA. The bus journey is exhilarating, always from high above, one moment huge bridge spans over the Caribbean, then viaducts over the islands, never a dull moment. There are famous names like Key Largo, and Marathon, but I left at Stock Island as Key West is fully booked for Fantasy Fest, and hired and erected a small tent on Boyd's Camping Ground, my home for two nights.

I spent the remainder of the evening with my feet dangling in the warm sea, drinking a beer called Yuengling, chatting to two delightful German au pairs, Natalie and Ruth, who were glorying in their one night off a week (and spending it with me!) We discussed Euro politics and the girls were happy to improve their English with me, as their employer's American English was, as we would describe, like double Dutch to them.

First thing in the morning I walk the length of Stock Island, and over the bridge onto Key West. I take a shuttle bus to the old town and wander the streets admiring the clapperboard houses and olde worlde charm, coupled with an air of chic. There is certainly a lot of colour here. After seeking out the bollard which claims to be the southernmost point of continental USA, 90 miles from Cuba. I make my way to the dock and board the catamaran Sebago. I've booked a little indulgent cruise.

There are about 30 tourists on board and four crew and we immediately set sail for the reef. Alison, an extremely scantily clad first officer makes her rounds fitting everyone with a wrist band. "That comes off with your first drink," she explains. Without the wristband you cannot drive the jet skis" Sounds fair enough.

But first there is the reef to negotiate. The seas are rather lumpy, and as we approach the reef you can see and hear the crashing white water as the ocean on the other side slams into the reef. Not ideal diving conditions! However, undeterred I don mask, snorkel and fins and jump in. As usual the water under the surge appears calm, and the fish simply bob up and down with the motion as indeed do I. Sadly, the reef, at least on lagoon side is mostly dead. There is some coral, but as I have witnessed on several occasions, the coral of the Caribbean is not thriving half so well as on the other side of the world, in the Indian Ocean. The only highlight is my encounter with a dozen or so wrasse, not unlike parrotfish with orange face and lips, iridescent blue necks, and dark blue bodies, and each is at least five feet in length and three feet from dorsal to belly. As I am struggling to observe, I drift a little too close to the reef and several waves threaten to impale me on the jagged outcrops. Feeling somewhat disoriented I kick back towards the boat and arrive safely after fighting the tide. Whilst I had been away the crew had cooked scrambled eggs and were now throwing the leftovers into the sea. I swam through a boiling feeding frenzy of yellow grunts to climb back aboard.

We sailed back towards the island eating a lunch of Southern fried chicken and prawns in a Cajun sauce, and docked at a raft to find our adventure equipment awaiting. First a speedboat was deployed and I went parasailing. Great fun in the Florida sunshine, especially with two gentle descents into the sea only to be lifted out at speed as the boat puts in a full throttle. Then they attached a banana boat to the speedboat and eight of us were thrown about, literally hanging on for grim death in another exercise in putting the fear of God up the tourist. Finally, I am handed the dead-man's key to my very own Jet ski. Ajay, a nervous young call centre operator from New Delhi asks if he can pillion. I'm happy to oblige and take him on a few high speed runs including tight turns. He thanks me profusely then begs to get off. On my own I exercise another series of adrenalin busting runs and eventually decide to call it a day. All of this merriment is way too much pleasure, and I should curb this delight in order to partake in drinks on deck. Alison cuts off my wrist band and breaks out the champagne.

The afternoon drifts lazily by, I may even have indulged in a gentle snooze, and we return to Key West dock. "You have two hours on land and then we set sail for the sunset cruise" announces the captain. "The best of Fantasy Fest can be found on Duval" she adds naughtily.

I wander around, feeling decidedly mellow, and eventually found a corner of Caroline and Duval to take in the carnival atmosphere. Leaning against a balustrade with Yeungling in hand I watch the antics of people I can only describe as exhibitionists whilst not in the least terming myself a voyeur.

There are folks, mainly couples, none under thirty, wandering around, or should I say parading themselves, in various states of undress, letting a variety of things hang out. But they are not just naturists for the sake of it. They are all sporting skimpy but well-designed outfits which show off their assets to their best. But not only that, they are all daubed in well-crafted body paint and appear marvellously eccentric. One moment I am standing next to two ample ladies, naked from the waist up, but you could not tell because their thickly applied body paint simply, how can I put it, adds to their bizarre countenance. There are other ladies who may or may not be wearing discreet coloured panties to augment their flamboyant body art, but you cannot be sure, and of course, a gentleman shouldn't look. But surely that is the reaction they want; and I am half pissed!

A painted pensioner is wearing nothing but a cowboy hat and a loin cloth which he merrily lifts to all passers-by to reveal…a remarkable colour scheme!

There is laughter and rock music everywhere, and everyone is having such an obviously good time, but eventually I have to leave this joyous scene to go for my sunset cruise. I wander away tipsily.

Alison welcomes me back on board the Sebago with a glass of champagne, and we sail away from the island and bob about on the ocean to watch the sun go down. It is a beautiful moment as the red sun sinks into the blue horizon and we are left with an evolving pink sky. We toast the sunset, and I re-join the clamour on Duval by nightfall, totally trolleyed and ready to further witness the crazy, raucous goings on.

There is a parade of floats, most of which contain men and women dressed as characters like Superwoman and Batman, and other gay icons. One float which looks like "Housewives of Key West" has ten dancing painted ladies and a lot of feathers. There are painted ghosts and ghouls, costumed animals, decorated phalluses, flashing lights and glitter galore. Everyone is laughing and dancing and having a good time. In a bar called Sloppy Joe's I spot shy, nervous Ajay, playing to the crowd and dancing around a pole sinking shots.

As I am talking to people, they are fascinated by my being British and my (naturally) English accent. Some ask if I work in the states, others if I have walked here...from England! I am asked if I know the Queen and the Beatles, and one lady said she loved Wales, London!

As the events begin to slow down, I am growing with confidence and begin to approach some Fantasy characters as if in an interview:

"Hello, I'm Geoff, from England, tell me, why have you come to Fantasy Fest today?"

I discover people here from Oregon, Wisconsin, Illinois, as well as locals. They are delighted to be interviewed by this stylish, intelligent, tea drinking "Londoner". They probably can't even detect I'm slurring. I illicit a variety of interesting responses.

"Oh Hi Geoff! I'm Amy, from Little Rock, Arkansas, and I've painted my breasts like a green dragon," and she thrusts accordingly.

"Yeah, I'm Natalie and this is Naomi, we're from Houston, Texas, and we've come as penis enlargers." They had large cockerels on their heads and a magnifying glass dangling from their nipple tassels. I moved on.

"Hey, you're from England. I'm Ben from Miami, and this is my wife Beth, and we are little devils" They had to be in their seventies and wore nothing but horned masks, red paint and pointy tails. I laughed and told them their costumes were absolutely wonderful. Beth looked at me askance and said, "Are you James Bond?"

Moving along the road as revellers headed home and the fast food stalls were closing up I spotted four cops standing on a grassy knoll, "Hi, I'm Geoff from England," I began and offered my outstretched hand.

Slam! The smaller cop, resembling Renko from Hill Street Blues, had, in a flash immobilised my arms, turned me around and forced me to my knees. Equally as quickly he stands me up and dusts me down. My flabber is totally ghasted! "We aren't your British Bobbies, you know, in the States you don't approach us, we approach you. Now on your way, Limey!" He drawls in a pseudo friendly, officious manner.

"Thank you, sorry!" I said, completely affirming one British stereotype. I was shaken, and not a little stirred. The encounter had completely sobered me up, so feeling just a little subdued, I found a taxi and asked to be returned to Boyd's.

Next morning, I crawled out of my tent and decided Dad had seen enough of Fantasy Fest and Las Vegas, and Utah and the Navajo Nation. Time to catch the Greyhound and go home.

*

A Central American Odyssey

The great continents of North and South America are linked by an isthmus which also separates the Atlantic and Pacific Oceans. This volatile area both politically and geologically is where the Mayan Indian ruled in pre-Colombian times. Now between Southern Mexico and Northern Colombia lie seven nations; Guatemala, Belize, Honduras, El Salvador, Nicaragua, Costa Rica and Panama. My adventures in the latter had wetted my appetite for the region, and I now embarked on a five country odyssey of discovery.

The beginning was a little convoluted, flights from Birmingham to Newark, (Wonderful views of the Arctic/Canadian icy wastes, the snow covered forests of New England, and the Manhattan skyline from the Hudson River approach) change for Houston where I am convinced we flew along the great Mississippi, then on through Mexico to Guatemala City, where I had booked a hotel in its neighbour, Antigua. It is no wonder I was confused and susceptible to a simple case of mistaken identity

Guatemala

Antigua is an old colonial town, nestled in a valley beside Guatemala City. It was the capital prior to erupting volcanoes, mudslides and earthquakes forcing a change of location.

I was quickly out of the baggage hall and through passport and customs, and there was a sign from my hotel, La Posada del Hermano Pedro (Brother Peter's Inn) being displayed by a driver. "Ok, si?" and Roland shrugged his acceptance and off we went. There was another name on the sign, Pulitzer, which I simply took as being the name of the taxi firm, as opposed to the literary prize.

It is dead of night, I am hoping to be at the hotel in time for a beer, I have already been travelling for 24 hours and I am aware the taxi is climbing a circuitous route up to a mountain pass to take me to the next valley. As we crest the ridge and begin our winding descent, Roland's mobile rings. At first he answers and speaks whilst still driving. I am aware the subject matter is a little more serious when he pulls over, looks at me and asks me my name, "Como se llama?"

"Señor Leo." I reply. "Es un problema?" I ask and he relays this information. There is a little more heated conversation and he puts the phone down, shrugs, mutters "No problema" and drives on.

In the morning, over breakfast I am introduced to Moira Pulitzer, a delightful young lady from Illinois who nonchalantly assures me that having to organise her own taxi from the airport (once she realised the hotel had left her high and dry, and following an embarrassing telephone conversation with the hotel) hadn't been a problem. I breakfasted sheepishly.

Prior to breakfast I had reconnoitred the town's main square, the Parque Central. Soon after dawn in the cooling shade of its ancient trees there were rows of people practising Tai Chi, commuters stopping off for a steaming mocha, and tourists like me, loitering by the old fountain, marvelling at the surrounding Spanish colonial architecture: old baroque with modern ice cream colours. Some of these churches date back to the early 16th century and have been ruined and rebuilt several times. There were six major earthquakes within 50 years of this city being founded. Perhaps someone was telling them something, the Indians certainly thought so.

Later I climbed to a mirador, the Cerro de la Cruz, a Christian shrine which had wonderful views of not only the town, but especially the three volcanoes which preside over the town, the volatile guardians which have forcibly shaped so much of Antigua's history. I lunched on a bocadillo in a comero, a local eatery, and lost my sunglasses, a reminder that in Central America anything that is put down belongs to all.

That evening, at 9pm, when my own body clock was at a sleep-deprived 2am, and over several beers in Mary's Bar (raucous and frequented mostly by Aussies) I chatted with Louiza, a tall blonde Spaniard ornithologist of Dutch descent. She told me about San Hermano Pedro (Saint Brother Peter) who is always depicted with a bell in which sits the infant Jesus. "It is where Babybel got their idea for baby cheeses" she joked. I received a further example of her dry humour when I asked how I could distinguish between the turkey buzzards and the black American vultures which constantly circle, "By the colour of their eyes!" she grinned. She was then very helpful with her generalisations of Central American peoples. "The Guatemalans are true Mayans, with their small stocky stature and flat faces. They eat small tortillas and refried beans. They hate the Mexicans and the Costa Ricans. Everybody hates the C.R.'s because they are so laid back and in bed with the Americans. The Hondurans cannot abide the Salvadoreans who hate them right back. They cannot even play a football match. In Panama and Costa Rica they eat bread, not tortillas, and in Nicaragua they eat gallo pinto, a mixture of rice and beans. In Belize they hate the Hondurans, just like everyone else." She continued like this for a while to remind me that this now predominantly peaceful region of the world has suffered vicious dictators, uprisings, wars and revolutions for centuries, with many atrocities committed, often in the name of those little round red blocks of cheese.

Before I left her, Louiza had one more nugget of enlightenment to share with me. "Hey, you know how the Machistos (she spat the word, she was quite drunk now), use powdered rhino horn, or shark fin, or eat turtle eggs as an aphrodisiac. We can stop this stupid trade. Just say only small men who are inadequate buy them. They will soon disappear." She crooked her little finger, laughed and took another swill of beer.

*

Lake Atitlan, in the highlands of Guatemala and the deepest in Central America, is also purportedly the most beautiful in the world, eclipsing Lake Como, according to Aldous Huxley who admired its setting surrounded by verdant volcanoes. Sadly, it is a dead lake. Whilst its fish stocks *should* be sustaining the 13 Mayan villages which occupy its shores, they must rely on agriculture alone. In the 1950's someone thought it would be a good idea to stock the lake with sport fish to promote tourism. Unfortunately, the black bass ate all of the indigenous fish, then were wiped out by the farming run off: pesticides and fertilizers and the like. Proof, if proof were needed, that you cannot interfere with fragile ecosystems. All ecosystems need to be self-sustaining, something best left to Mother Nature alone.

I had arrived in Panajachel (known as Pana) and was taken by speedboat across to the main village of Santiago Atitlan where I reluctantly tackled a steep hill to a private house in order to meet the minor deity, Maximon. He is a limbless (due to infidelity) cigar smoking, alcohol swilling effigy who is moved from house to house by a brotherhood devoted to the idol's wellbeing. Maximon is a fusion of Mayan culture, Christianity and conquistador legend, typical of the conflated religious position of much of Latin America. There is currently a form of backlash against the traditional fire and brimstone preaching of Roman Catholicism, and filling the resultant void are not only gods like Maximon, but also the ominous North American Evangelist preachers who promise a much easier passage to Paradise.

Antigua suffered greatly during the Guatemalan Civil War, fuelled in the second half of the twentieth century by the USA's paranoia over communism succeeding in its "own back yard". Indigenous peoples were seen as leftist opponents to the Government and there were many hundreds of disappearances and other atrocities. Another example of messing with fragile ecosystems. When will they learn?

My day relaxing on the shores of Lake Atitlan ended early as I continued to catch up on lost sleep. It was followed by a dawn to dusk drive via the colourful market town of Chichicastenango, to Honduras and the town of Copan which houses the ruins of a whole Mayan community.

Honduras

After the border we meet a quintessentially Honduran sight. This poorest of the Central American countries has young boys who stand at the side of the road holding 4-foot-long iguanas by the tail, offering them for sale. They make good soup, I was assured. Nothing too unusual about that, but those who don't own an iguana will dig potholes into the Pan American Highway then stand dolefully next to their handiwork with their hands begging for donations so they can then repair their own creations. Traffic has to wildly zigzag about to avoid this wanton vandalism for which the authorities have no solution. Progress through Honduras is slow indeed. Sometimes they repair the potholes with grass. If there's one thing the suspension of a car needs less than traffic-calming humps, it's potholes dressed as divots.

I spent a whole day in Copan Ruinas, clambering around the acropolis, temples, pyramids, tombs, tunnels, ball courts and sculptures; and marvelling at the hieroglyphs and numerous stelae, and then its museum, before exploring the surrounding woods for ruins of homesteads, outhouses and other evidence of habitation. Coatis scuttle and Macaws swoop and caw endlessly as I wander through these artefacts of a civilisation so different to sites I'd seen on other continents.

There, below the town was the meandering river which sustained it prior to being virtually abandoned before the conquistadores arrived. With rulers like Smoke Monkey, Moon Jaguar and 18 Rabbit, and a supposed suicidal game of football, this was a strange place indeed. I'm not convinced by the theories about this ballgame. For a start it was a game played in a court where any part of the body could be used, except the hands or feet; archaeologists suggest players could hip or thigh the ball into the goal. Well, that is as maybe, but the next assertion doesn't bear fruit for me. The gods they worshipped, and who had to be appeased by sacrifice should nature or enemies conspire against them, had to be kept strong. Therefore, they needed regular new blood. Thus, so the theory goes, how better to keep their gods fit and healthy than to offer them the greatest of their athletes. Consequently, whichever teams won the games were sacrificed to join the gods. If there's a more apt definition of irony, I'd like to hear it – talk about positive discrimination. It reminded me of a Kurt Vonnegut story, *Harrison Bergeron*, where – in a dystopian future world – everyone is handicapped by the government to ensure that no one excels in any field. I think the athletes would have welcomed an enforced handicap over martyrdom. I bet selection meetings were interesting. My guess is that there were an awful lot of no-score draws…

So, either the Mayans told the conquistadores these preposterous rules in order to appear strong and fearless, with powerful gods, or the Spaniards made it up so they could justify their genocide of such an 'uncivilised race'.

I spent an hour before dinner visiting a zoo called Macaw Mountain which had lots of colourful birds, butterflies and huge spiders. The next morning, I encountered some American evangelical missionaries over breakfast, all teeth and hair. One woman greeted everybody with an extremely elongated and loud "Buaynose Deeeyaarse, Hiiiiiyaaaaa!

Talk about uncivilised races. I wonder if she could score a goal with her thigh…

El Salvador

I travel around. It's what I do, so if I find myself in a hotel for more than a couple of nights, I get itchy feet. For this reason, I tend to stay in fairly simple, cheap hotels, hostels or even dorms. And I am able to plan ahead, using the internet and a variety of search sites, I can have a look at where I'll plan to be tomorrow, and book a room accordingly. This is unlike my literary hero, Bill Bryson, half of whose adventures - taking his notes from Small Islands or Big Countries - involved searching on foot or with public transport for a reasonable bed for the night. This is why it was unusual to find myself in Suchitoto in El Salvador at quite the most exquisite hotel you can imagine.

The Hotel Almendros de San Lorenzo is a beautifully appointed hacienda with furniture and ornaments, artefacts and objets d'art gleaned and garnered worldwide. There is not a book out of place, nor any marble, sculpture, glass, pot, plant, picture or polished wooden statue that looked in the least incongruous. The whole interior; reception, library, corridors purred with harmony and oozed quiet, subdued, silken opulence. The fragrant tropical gardens, its furniture and water features were decadent to say the least; the views down to the lake and across to the mountains personified succulence. This wasn't what I was used to, and certainly not what I had paid for. Then I was shown to my room; a suite on two floors as thoughtfully furnished as the whole hotel with jacuzzi and private balcony overlooking everything. I think they must have confused me with a Russian oligarch, because this room was surely beyond my means and certainly beyond my comprehension.

I had also been impressed as I travelled throughout El Salvador, a small, beautiful country with such a troubled past and people who had suffered wars, atrocities and forced migration, and who were now rebuilding with such innocence and vigour. The same old story: peasants forced to work for evil, corrupt landowners then labelled as communists and treated like terrorists when they rise up for just a small degree of justice.

Suchitoto is the country's cultural centre, and an atmospheric old colonial town with the sort of town square where you could sit and hope that time would stand still. When I wrenched myself away from the hotel, and had finished wandering the cobbled streets, I sat in the square drinking beer, eating pupusas (traditional Salvadorean tortillas filled with cheese, beans, or meat), admiring the old white church, and enjoying the antics of a flock of swallows which had made the eaves of the church their home, swarming and swooping at the end of a long day of insect catching and fledgling feeding. It was akin to a murmuration of starlings, their aerial acrobatics.

On my second morning as I sprawled across a sofa in reception awaiting a guide and settling into the ambience of the history of the displays, like sinking into a warm bath, two men arrived to register. The first, a wizened wiry man in his late sixties, spoke in an Australian accent.

"Yeah, I originally booked a double room, because my wife was staying, but I'm not meeting up with her now, so I'm travelling with Mr Davies here, so we'll need a twin room."

Quite rational, so I thought, it is not unreasonable for travellers to double up and share the costs of expensive hotels. And I know I shouldn't have been listening in, but then the desk clerk, who I was guessing may have been one of the owners, had a different take on things.

"Eet ees OK," he smiled, "In Salvador we are very liberated and there is no need to worry, you can still have the double room."

"No, we want a room with twin beds, please" insisted the Aussie.

"But eet ees no longer against the law, we are quite 'appy to accommodate you in a double room."

The Englishman, in his 40's and bespectacled piped up; "Oh. I see what you are thinking, no, we are not gay, and we have nothing against the gay community either, we are just travelling companions, so we need single beds."

"There is no need any more in El Salvador to pretend," the receptionist continued to smile and patronise the couple, "we now are a very emancipated nation and you are allowed to have a hotel room together. However, if you insist on single beds, then that can be arranged."

"But we're not gay!" spluttered the Australian. The receptionist, however had already tinkled his little bell and was giving instructions in Spanish to the porter who picked up their bags and gave the exasperated couple a smile and a wink and beckoned them to follow.

I later met up with Gavin and Adrian for dinner and beers in the town square and with lively music blaring from every lamp post, they had some interesting tales to tell.

Gavin was a West Australian bush ranger now, but previously had been brought up and worked in Zimbabwe as a policeman in the early 60's, when it was still Southern Rhodesia.

"One night, we were called to a burglary at the house of a politician in the suburbs of a black township and we arrived just as the gang were making their getaway into the bush. Now, in those days you shouted a warning, and if the scoundrels wouldn't stop you raised your gun, aimed and fired regardless. I had this black man in my sights but hesitated and he ran off but was apprehended by a colleague a little later on. I'll always remember his name, Robert Mugabe.

I often think, if only I had been a little more positive, who knows ...."

Adrian's tale was much more recent, November 1997. "I was with a group of tourists in Luxor, Egypt and we were on an excursion where, after visiting the Valley of the Kings, you rode by donkey up and out of the valley, then down to the Temple Of Hatshupset. There were twelve of us so we needed 12 donkeys, but at the last minute a young girl had joined us so we needed to wait for a 13th donkey. We were told it would be just a few minutes, but typical Egyptian time, it took over an hour to secure another donkey before we could begin the trek. We went up through the saddle and could see the beautiful marble temple below us. Slowly the donkeys descended and we were half way down the mountain when we heard the gunshots, screams and explosions, and our guides quickly diverted us away from the scene. It was only later that we realised we had avoided the massacre in which over 60 people, mainly tourists were slaughtered. The Thirteenth Donkey; Lucky for some!"

Suchitoto is a bird watcher's paradise, and I had already enjoyed sharing my breakfast on the terrace with a turquoise browed mot-mot, the national bird, and several tiny humming birds. My journey that morning was a boat trip around Lago Suchitlan. There were half a dozen of us, including the recent arrivals, and we were greeted on the jetty by the toothless grin of a bronzed boatman. We clambered in and were immediately engulfed by a swarm of huge black flying beetles. There was some consternation and not a little swatting. "Don't worry!" cried the boatman above the sound of the outboard motor, "They are friends of men, Amigos de Hombres. They don't bite us, only horses."

Reassured we continued and were served up a twitcher's feast. Up in the trees and in amongst the reeds we saw swallows, egrets, osprey, falcons, kingfishers, herons, kiskadees, flycatchers, coots, ducks, orioles, and many more;

and all around wonderful views of green mountains and more smoking volcanoes of the ring of fire.

The water was bright blue with an algae bloom, and after skirting some islands the boatman took us toward an inlet in which the water appeared black. As we came closer we could see that on the water floated thousands of cormorants, some stood on logs with their wings spread toward the sun for drying. With our craft approaching the flock took flight. There was thunderous splashing as they beat against the water to get airborne, but once up they stayed close to the surface. Suddenly we were in amongst them and surrounded on all sides. You could feel the wind and hear the noise from their beating wings. The air was alive with countless birds, mostly flying parallel to the boat. If you extended your arm you could almost touch the tip of their expansive wings. For the next few minutes you could do naught but marvel at their majesty. I was thinking, what was it about Central American lakes which could sustain millions of birds, but not facilitate a fishing industry? No I wasn't. I was totally lost in the moment, awestruck. The thinking came later.

After lunch I decided to walk to a local waterfall, revered for its beauty. I had to enlist the help of the tourist police. Suchitoto is perfectly safe, I was assured, but the next town is controlled by gangs who sometimes go in for a little kidnapping.

Juan and Jose accompanied me, and on the journey I showed them my photographs of the lake and surrounding mountains next to a picture of my back garden the day I left: bare branches and a lawn covered in frost and snow. They appeared slightly envious; "Mmm, nice and cool!" they seemed to say. As we walked on through fragrant, sun kissed meadows and woodland I tried to teach the two boys a phrase; "This job's a doddle!"

The waterfall was a delightful place, if mostly dry with hexagonal basalt columns which I had only previously seen on the Devil's Causeway in Northern Ireland. Those are some of the oldest rocks in the world while these must be some of the newest. Tomorrow: Nicaragua.

I was sad to leave El Salvador, which, at the risk of sounding patronising, I found to be an optimistic country, full of Neuva Esperanza, the title of some villages being repopulated and reawakened by returning refugees, the diaspora. "New Hope!"

Nicaragua

After a long drive I arrived at the city of Leon. Too late to take it in, and after dinner, bed and breakfast in a utilitarian hotel, I left to undertake a volcano adventure.

I had decided to climb Cerro Negro, Nicaragua's newest volcano. It is in the active range that joins Nicaragua's most famous puffing Billy of a volcano, San Cristobal in the North to La Pelona further East. This is where the Pacific plate meets the Atlantic plate and is pushing up to create this line of fire.

It is great fun climbing volcanoes because of the heat, loose clinker, smell of sulphur, and threat of eruption. There's always something going on. You stare down holes that lead to hell yet admire vistas which are heavenly. The real excitement though is in the lee of the mountain, which is sheltered from the prevailing wind and therefore the soot, dust and ash settles to create a very thick but soft layer.

I was with a group that zigzagged up the mountain in searing heat and with a hot wind taking the skin from our faces. As we mounted ridges near the summit it felt like we could be carried on the wind like fragments of ash. There was loose terrain underfoot, much of which was like cannonballs which had been ejected from the caldera. Many of the group suffered slips and falls, but I was confident of my own surefootedness; until I trod on a cannonball and stumbled. It was a small stumble and I felt I could easily correct it, until I stumbled onto another cannonball and suddenly my plight began to take on more worrying proportions. In slow motion, both legs and arms were flailing as I struggled to maintain control. Judith, an accountant from Leeds, happened to be walking next to me and instinctively reached out to try to steady me: I eagerly grabbed for her. Unfortunately, my right arm missed her completely and the other reached out grasping in panic; and my left hand grabbed onto the first thing it could. It was soft and squidgy but solid enough for me to stop struggling and pull myself upright. It was only as my head cleared from the panic I realised I was holding onto Judith's right breast.

"Aagh!" I exclaimed, looking at my errant hand as if it didn't belong to me, then "Ooh!" as I hurriedly let go and pulled my arm away as if I were holding a smouldering hot coal. "I am sooo sorry! I don't know what happened, I never meant to er, you know," I apologised most profusely.

"It's ok," Judith laughed, "It was an accident, no harm done." I was relieved at her amused take on matters, she could have justifiably adopted an indignant stance to the Carry On incident.

And now to the descent. This is something I learned to do on the slopes of Vulcano, in the Italian Aolian Islands, north of Sicily. I shouted to everyone, "Don't worry, just follow me!" And from the summit I launched into a galumphing run down the mountain. The soft sediment takes your weight like quicksand, but doesn't hold on, so each wild stride can take you ten yards in a dizzying plunge. It is impossible to stop, so you find yourself terribly out of breath because of your windmilling legs, and then finally, as the slope evens out you come gradually to a heart racing, lung breaking stop, and can do little else but collapse into a heap of uncontrollable fits of laughter. The whole process takes less than two minutes to come down from an ascent which took over two hours. Some people do it on sledges. That was Cerro Negro, the Black Hill.

Returning to Leon, I had time to take in the city. It is dominated by its huge, white, colonial style cathedral. Some believe it was originally intended for the capital city of Peru, Lima, but come what may it ended up here. Inside is a cavernous cool space dominated by the biggest "Stations Of The Cross" canvases I had ever seen. Each of the fourteen stations was

exquisitely painted arched depictions of scenes from Holy Week.

I spent a couple of hours wandering and admiring the Basilica of the Assumption of the Blessed Virgin Mary and its art and statuary before paying to ascend to the roof and receiving marvellous views of the city and its surroundings. However, I had to return inside to spend more time with the saddest, most doleful marble lion which commemorates the resting place of Nicaragua's favourite poet, Ruben Dario.

I returned to Leon's stifling streets to discover a sleepy market, but it was not long before I had to dive into an air conditioned museum. Firstly, a delightfully shaded courtyard with a sprinkling fountain, coolness personified, then I plunged into the galleries. You always get pleasing and uplifting surprises from any museum, anywhere in the world, and here was no exception. Among the early Mayan artefacts and revolutionary reminders, I came across a Picasso; *Dos Acrobates y un Perro* quite lovely. As I wandered the cool rooms I was pleased to note each room must have had motion sensors, for as I entered, the lights would flicker on and the fountains would begin to sprinkle, then as I left all would return to dark silence, very modern, very technological. It was only after some time of this, and with some little embarrassment that I realised I was being quietly followed into each room by the curator who would switch on the electrics, and who dutifully turned everything off as I left.

The next morning began with a power cut, so I set off to find a bakery which hopefully had baked breakfast products prior to the blackout. Having taken coffee and croissants I decided I would leave for Granada, but not before visiting the beautiful ice cream, mango and pink exterior of the church of Jesus of Calvary at the top of the hill behind the cathedral. As I approached I could hear the chanting of a mass in progress, and could see people entering and leaving quite smartly as they popped by for a quick confession on their way to work. The huge doors were agape and I similarly entered -gape mouthed - to see a gargantuan depiction of the crucifixion flanked by enormous crucified robbers. Looking up rather than ahead, I stubbed my big toe on the stone portal and winced and fell into the church, "Shit!" I exclaimed, and immediately shrank as priests looked up and the congregation turned to witness my plight. "Sorry!" I mouthed as I reversed out of the church and sat on a step to nurse my stricken foot.

The road to Granada took me via Managua, the nation's capital city. I briefly stopped to see the huge Old Cathedral Square, built in revolutionary times to accommodate propaganda rallies, now eerily empty, characterless and silent. I quickly moved on for I was excited to see Masaya, Nicaragua's first and largest national park and one of its foremost tourist attractions, an active volcano 20 kilometres south of the city.

The visitor centre was well appointed and very informative, and a worthwhile taster. Then there was the drive by minibus through the black lava fields of unsettling, contorted basaltic formations, to the edge of the caldera. And here you had a huge hole in the ground, the "entrance to hell", where you lean over the small protective wall to see directly into the cone of an active volcano, a crater hundreds of metres across and, deep inside, a lake and hundreds of fumaroles venting and degassing from the molten mass below. Sadly, as a result of this, the potentially spectacular view was veiled by smoke. As keenly as you peered into the massive hole, there was nothing to reward your efforts but white smoke, not even swirling, just steam, and the acrid stench of sulphur. All in all, I couldn't decide whether it was the least impressive thing I had ever seen or the most disappointingly impressive thing I had ever seen, either way I understood why the visitor centre had to be so visually informative.

And on to Granada, on the shores of Lake Nicaragua, and the first official town of the whole Americas. The lake has access to the Caribbean via the San Juan river, and is not far from the Pacific, so many of the first visionaries saw this as the sight of the canal which could join the two oceans and remove the need for the perilous and expensive journey around Cape Horn. Sadly, it was Granada's access from the Caribbean which caused it to be much plundered by pirates in its early history. Firstly, Henry Morgan and then a particularly nasty character (not that Morgan was anything of a saint) by the name of William Walker who razed Granada with his followers called Filibusters. Walker was an adventurer and privateer whose vision for the region was the creation of new slave states. He briefly became president of Nicaragua partly supported by the US, but when defeated by Honduran, Salvadorean and Costa Rican troops he retreated and burned Granada. He was later disowned by America, captured by the British and delivered to the Hondurans who had him executed in 1860.

Here, there is a vibrant tree-lined town park next to the beautiful mango cathedral. There are pedestrianised tourist areas and each building has a garden courtyard, the gates to which are high and wide to allow horses to enter directly before their riders would dismount.

I climbed the bell tower of the church of Our Lady of Mercy for wonderful views over the terracotta roofs of the town, and to the south the cloud forested volcano, Mombacho, with Lake Nicaragua and Las Isletas to the East. I then walked to the lakeside, water always lures me in. It was disappointingly run down with boarded shops and derelict buildings. Wild horses grazed on the thin beach grass, and the flat floodplain was so strewn and carpeted with plastic carrier bags inflated by the constant breeze that it resembled a giant, multi-coloured bubble-wrap. Undeterred I took a boat out to a peninsular of islets which are homes to wealthy foreigners, but more importantly to magnificent bird life. Ospreys and egrets, magpie-jays and kingfishers, weavers and Jesus birds (Northern Jacana, they walk on water), and the wonderfully named and beautifully coloured Montezuma Oropendola, among many others. There was a fort built to ward off pirates like Morgan, and monkeys galore, but my highlight was the cloud of swooping, swirling swallows devouring the clouds of biting insects

Granada is vibrant in the evening with mariachi bands wandering among the outdoor diners. I loved watching one such quartet begin serenading a rich, drunk American whose bald obesity most resembled Jabba the Hut. He fell sound asleep and the band grew louder and louder and eventually hugely discordant in their efforts to revive the slumbering tip giver. They failed and left dispirited, El Condor Pasa!

There is an immediate feel for the rivalry between these twin university cities of Leon and Granada which sandwich Managua. Leon is hot and dry, liberal, lyrical, a place of poetry, art and music. Granada is cooler by the lakeside, but flyblown, its flamboyance of architecture hides a serious, militaristic and political side. Today, sadly it is a centre for rich Americans to exploit the sex trade.

After breakfast I was heading for the Pacific coast but first had chance to dive into Mi Museo, attached to the cathedral. Here there were galleries composed of tableaux depicting effigies of dominant pre-Columbian, first millennium, Pacific plains women. Found amongst burial grounds, these early bronze artefacts with their distended bellies also had something of Jabba the Hut about them.

I decided I could do with a few days at the seaside, so hopped on a Ticabus and made my way to Nicaragua's most popular Pacific Ocean beach resort, San Juan del Sur. Not that I am a complete beach freak, but mainly I wanted to see the turtles which spawn, nest and hatch just a few kilometres up the coast. Arriving at this perfectly curved bay the first thing you see, and therefore becomes the first thing you must visit, is the huge statue of Christ which dominates the hill overlooking the bay to the North. Barely could I set my backpack down, in the Hotel Colonial, one street back from the beach, then I set off on the trek.

I began along the beach, past gelaterias, bars and restaurants until I came to a rickety peaton (pedestrian only) suspension bridge. Then the climb started, firstly through condominium land, and past pleasanter haciendas until the road wound behind the hill and eventually up to the shrine. There were marvellous views in every direction, especially back into the San Juan bay with its curve of white sand, its little boats bobbing and the sea looking the warmest and most welcoming azure blue. Christ himself was a much smaller version of Brazil's Christ the Redeemer (125 feet) on Il Corcovado, and with only one arm outstretched pointing South. He looked old, a state, of course He never achieved. His title is El Cristo Sagrado Misericordia, which sounds like he looks, miserable, but stands for Christ of Mercy. I heard an American tourist actually say "It's like a mini Rio here!" Well, no.

I spent some time admiring the views and looking around the chapel carved into the rock beneath the statue, before descending to the rickety suspension bridge. Behind this I had noticed an area of fresh water mangrove which I decided to explore. After spotting a pair of Jesus birds, which I thought rather appropriate, I came to a clearing and a bare-chested local lad leapt up to greet me.

"Buenas" he greeted warmly, "I am William; Americano?" he asked, obviously hoping for rich pickings.

"No, no, soy Ingles" I replied in perfect Spanish. As he shook my hand vigorously with his right, I couldn't help noticing that he grasped a machete with his left hand, and he was not about to put it down, as I thought one might do in polite company.

"Aah! Manchester United!" he grinned, still shaking my hand strongly.

I grinned similarly and nodded. "Er, soy tarde para bus" I said nervously, still grinning, but pointing back towards the road, hoping I had told him I was late for my bus.

"Ok, adios" he said, and let me go and we parted amicably.

You always have to be careful, of course, wherever in the world you are, even in your own back garden, and travelling alone means; one, you have to be a little more vigilant and aware, and; two, you rapidly become paranoid about being vigilant and aware.

You hear stories of people who get into the wrong taxi, are driven out of town, stripped and beaten, then forced to reveal card pin numbers. William was different. After all, he didn't claim to drive a taxi, nor offer to take me anywhere. He could just have been the local village psycho with a machete. The paranoia always involves machetes. The upshot is that you tend not to meet as many people as you would like, and taxi drivers think you are mad when you run away from them.

Returning to the hotel, I donned my swimming trunks and grabbed a towel for my dip in the warm and welcoming azure waters. Yes, I went for a swim, a pleasure I shared with the pelicans, but the sea here is cold. How can this be? We are in equatorial climes, not very far from the warm Caribbean. The answer lies in the currents. The Pacific swirls anti clockwise and the Humboldt Current flows all the way up from Antarctica, past the coastline of South America, and as I discovered, at least as far as here. This is why the fishing industry is so important here, the rich nutrient filled ocean is perfect for shoals of herring. This is why there are penguins and seals in the Galapagos Islands, practically on the equator. This is why whales choose this shoreline to follow on their birthing migrations. And this is why my dip was necessarily curtailed.

I wanted to see turtles. Behind the beach I found a tourist information office, and inside met Gordon. Gordon was an affable, bearded young man from Buxton in Derbyshire. He told me that yes, it was possible to take a trip to La Flor Beach Natural Reserve where the Olive Ridley turtles come to lay during a period called Arribada, but unfortunately they had laid a fortnight ago, and with a gestation period of 45 days, I had arrived in San Juan del Sur at just the wrong time. (as usual). Once again the old adage had come true; "If you want to go on safari to see wonderful wildlife, don't follow Leo".

It was while researching (Googling) Gordon's office that I came across this BBC headline; "Robbery of 18 tourists at gunpoint on night tour - San Juan del Sur". I just hope it wasn't William.

I had another day in San Juan which meant two nights wining and dining in the excellent Iguana Bar, right on the ocean, sipping margaritas at two for $5. Well, it would be rude not to. During a chance conversation in the Iguana, I learned about the twin volcano island of Ometeppe in Lake Nicaragua, and a hotel called Charco Verde (green puddle) located actually within the Nature reserve. I decided to postpone Costa Rica. It can wait a few more days, I thought.

It was an all-day drive to the town of Rivas, a busy market town, capital of this region, and I had to fight off two sharks, one with a faked taxi sign and a dirty, screwed up picture of a hotel ripped from a magazine. "Five dollar, five dollar," he repeatedly shouted at me. Luckily I had booked a small room in the Hostal Lydia ahead of my arrival. The security guard at the petrol station directed me.

Wandering around the town square which had an extremely pretty church, I was a little disconcerted with the repeated shouts of "Blanco" from some youths who appeared to be shadowing me. I kept to the main roads. A crowd had gathered, and I joined, as you do, and an ambulance arrived noisily. Some poor lad had come off his motorbike and broken his leg.

An early night in my windowless room in Lydia, which opened onto a courtyard and crowded garden. There were toilets with outdoor sinks. A silver haired lady dressed all in black, rocked gently in her chair and gazed at the grainy little television set sat on a high cupboard. She gave me a toothless grin as her daughter asked about my breakfast requirements. I was to take the 7am ferry from San Jorge, so she said she would arrange for a taxi, an early call, and food and coffee.

The ferry took two hours to Moyogalpa, capital of Ometeppe, and with every minute the twin peaks, permanently hatted, drew closer and more and more exciting. My adventure on Charco Verde was about to begin.

I walked off the ferry with a dozen or so fellow passengers, followed by a couple of delivery vehicles. It was uphill, of course and I passed a few shops, hostels and cafes before coming to a tree in front of the small white church at the top of the town. The shade of the tree was very welcoming as I sat contemplating how to get to Charco Verde. On the map it looked just a short walk from the town, but enquiries at the local coffee house told me it was nearly ten miles. There are two roads on the island, each looping around a volcano like a sideways figure of eight. My destination was a quarter around the fat half of the eight, facing south.

I would take the bus.

A little about local buses in Central America. Known universally as "Chicken buses", they are antiquarian and battered, displaying chrome, Jesus stickers, statues and mobiles. Mostly they are second-hand school buses from the U.S. which have been pimped, Latin American style. Everything (people, animals, worldly goods) goes inside until crammed to overflowing; then it goes on top. There is no such thing as full. There is no timetable, the driver simply waits for his lunch to go down, or whichever meal he is lazily consuming, everyone to load up who wants to go somewhere, then sets off when he's finished chatting. It is no good seeing an empty bus idling beneath a tree and thinking "Ooh, I'll leap on and off we'll go!" It could be another hour before it leaves.

Once on the bus and bouncing around on the pitted roads a teenage boy suddenly appears from nowhere and starts taking fares from all the passengers. However crowded, he will squeeze himself around seated and standing passengers and their cargo, waving a wad of dirty notes, adding to and dispensing change as he writhes and shouts above the cacophony of laughter and conversation. It is hot and smelly, but not sweaty smelly, simply the accumulation of people and animals and time and the land. It is an honest smell, an earthy smell, with faint traces of wood smoke, tobacco, greenery and toil.

And then the bus will lurch to a halt and the boy is shouting "Charco Verde, Charco Verde", and looking at me and nodding. "This," I reason, "is where the gringo gets off."

I am deposited at the side of the road, there is a gateway and a dirt track leading down through an avenue of trees and scrub. Beyond there are some scattered low buildings (including my bed for the night, I imagined) and the blue, glistening lake. Behind me looms the active peak called Concepcion (5250 feet). I heave my back pack on and set off down the track.

The place is quite beautiful. As I stride on, skittish lizards who have been warming in the sunshine skitter into the dry undergrowth, turkey buzzards circle, and howler monkeys howl. The trees here are full of howler families. Ever present magpie jays (crested and much bigger and better plumaged than our magpies) squawk their warnings as they appear to follow me down the path. There is the hum of bees and other insects reminiscent of an English summer meadow, but the shrill ringing of cicadas remind you that you are far, far from home.

After half an hour I arrive at the hotel and begin to settle in. At the shore the clear water gently laps onto a thin beach of black sand, to left and right the forest comes right down to the water and dips leaves and branches. Snowy egrets perch upright. I see a horse happily bathing, waist deep, evidently relaxing after a busy morning on the farm. Beyond the horse a couple of fishermen are casting nets. Next to some sun loungers there is an open building which doubles as bar and restaurant, and behind the trees to my left is a row of brightly coloured wooden chalets each with a hammock slung across the porch. Every shrub and tree in the cultivated gardens flowers with brightly coloured blooms matching the painted cabanas, and the first one is mine.

What to do first, swim or explore. The lake is inviting, calm, warm and of course, fresh water. It wins. I had read that long ago bull sharks had navigated from the Caribbean up the San Juan river and settled and bred in the lake. No one had seen the "devil fish" in years, but these thoughts naturally invade any fertile mind when you can't see *what might lurk below.*

Charco Verde advertises itself as an ecological park, a biosphere of Ometepe, and the flora and fauna are indeed diverse and beautiful, as are the views around the lake, the lagoon, and of course the volcanoes; Concepcion and Maderas, the latter being slightly smaller and dormant. Both have forested slopes with clouded peaks.

I was eager to discover the miles of forest trails, keen to observe the wildlife, and especially as I had allocated several days for exploration, I wanted to see how it changed at different times of the day. How did dusk differ to dawn, and the times in between. So I swam, took lunch (uninspiring), dozed in my hammock, then attacked the trails. By late afternoon I had exhausted the trail around the lagoon, the trail to the highpoint, with superb 360 views, the beach trail of flotsam and jetsam, and trails through both meadows and forest. Finally, I lounged by the beach and watched the most superb sunset. A long day is over and nightfall brings only the prospect of dinner, and going by lunch that will be more an endurance than a pleasure. There are few other guests and the staff appear bored to the point of surly. Thank goodness for beer and a good book.

My dawn walk reveals nothing new, and either side of breakfast I have completed all trails for a second time. I decide to return to Moyogalpa to check ferry times, take lunch and be amongst people again. On the main track I spot a comeda where I can walk for dinner later, and I also wander into a tiny community of shacks where children are playing in the dust, the Lambada is blasting out from behind a curtain, there's a half-hearted shop with a table offering sparsely displayed misshapen fruit and vegetables, and two men are throwing sticks up a tree trying to dislodge an iguana for the pot. It all seems a rather poor and pitiable existence, and not for the first time do I feel like a bloated, over-privileged voyeur. But everyone still smiles their "Buenas".

Returning to Charco Verde there are some American day trippers and German cyclists who wander around the grounds chatting loudly, pointing excitedly at the monkeys and generally looking down on staff and guests, as they are merely "passing through". No wonder the staff appear disinterested. People arrive, take lunch, then leave, with little conception of the lives of those who eke out an existence here.. As a resident I realise I am also being observed, pointed at, talked about, even photographed. I have become part of the tourism zoo. "Look at the local, lying in his hammock!" I hum the Lambada and doze in the sunshine, dreaming of iguana soup.

I set off for the comeda at around seven. It is pitch black with no street lighting, of course, and with maybe a half moon, the stars and my head torch. It is only a couple of miles to the little village where I plan to eat, but things appear vastly different at night. The ringing of the cicadas has been replaced by the chirping of frogs, and the trees whose shadows are welcome during the day to protect from the searing sun now become eerily dark shapes potentially hiding potholes and pitfalls. I begin to realise I am an easy target for opportunistic peasants. People here aren't criminally minded, but with empty stomachs and hardly a centavo to rub together, when some foolhardy western tourist homes into view on a lonely track, well…

Once spooked, the mind goes into overdrive. Nobody knows you're here, and I stride on, but then falter when the next scenario hits me. I'm in the village, at the local eatery, fed well with a few beers inside me, show my wallet to pay the bill, then leave unaccompanied to wander beerily down the track. That's the time a couple of enthusiastic youths could jump me. I stop, look around me at the shadows and isolation, hesitate, then rather ashamedly turn on my heels and walk back towards the hotel. Discretion, I assure myself, is always the better part of valour.

Back at the hotel, feeling rather sorry for myself (some bloody adventurer, me!) I dine on chicken and potatoes again, take a few beers and read my book. When, at around ten I get up for another beer, I notice I am left alone. Even the bar staff have gone to bed. I turn off the lights, lock up and cross the garden to my cabana. Tomorrow, Costa Rica.

About three in the morning I woke up, desperate for the toilet. I didn't bother with the light, but as I crossed the bedroom floor I trod on what seemed to be a twig. Once in the bathroom with the light on, I notice that the bottom of my foot is a bit sticky (no pun intended). Returning I turn on the bedroom light and there, stuck to the floor by its squashed tail, is a scorpion. Lucky escape for me, if not for the scorpion.

In the morning there is a line of ants joining the scorpion's empty shell to the gap beneath my door. After dressing I open the door to reveal the glowing light of dawn. Dawn is a little late here as the sun has to climb above the imposing height of Concepcion. The night time geckos have vanished from the white walls, but the sounds of morning; cicadas, magpie jays, and howler monkeys, fill the air. I sit on my hammock and bend to put on my boots which I have foolishly left outside overnight. With the thoughts of hidden scorpions in my mind I bang my boots on the floor, and a huge spider flops out and scuttles away under the adobe wall. After the initial shock, an overwhelming feeling of relief washes over me. Relief that today, straight after breakfast, I am leaving Charco Verde.

I walked for two hours before breakfast, constantly accompanied by the ubiquitous magpie jays squawking, whistling, hooting and burbling; "Look at me...Look at me!" As I walked up to the mirador, down to the lagoon, east to the promontory, and back along the beach, there were butterflies and burrowing wasps, bats returning from the night hunt, dung beetles and armies of leaf cutter ants, busily at work even at this unearthly hour. At the shore were herons, egrets, jakartas and pygmy doves. In the trees, kiskadees and a beautiful mot-mot, and families of monkeys. I strolled, marvelling at the nature surrounding me and pondered my destiny.

As the waiter delivered my pancakes for breakfast he smiled and asked, "What is your destiny today?" Spooky, has he been in my mind?

One thought invades as I take the ferry back to the mainland. Three large lakes I had been on in Central America, and previously Lake Gatun in Panama, and apart from the sight of a few net casting wading fishermen, there appeared to be no fishing industry. Neither were there any pleasure craft; yachts and dinghies, even speed boats and water skiers, no jet skiers (thank goodness). It all seemed rather lifeless and underused.

I disembark at San Jorge into a cloud of mosquitos, then taxi up to the main road in Rivas to take the bus to Costa Rica. At the gas station which acts as bus stop there are a few plastic chairs facing a television showing a live game of football from Anfield. Wow, it is the evening kick off in England between Liverpool and Man City. The score is two all, and the match is nearing its conclusion. An elderly American takes the seat next to me. "You watching the Superbowl?" he drawls.

"No, I'm afraid I don't know anything about American football, this is football" I replied politely.

He's a 70-year-old thin man with a shock of grey hair, wearing a dark suit jacket but jogging bottoms and sporting both a baseball cap and trainers.

"Is that an Aussie English accent or a British English accent?" he asks.

"No, It is an English English accent" I corrected him.

He looks up at the screen, "And this is British Football?"

"No," I was becoming a little exasperated. "This is English football, the Premier League from England" I felt a little sheepish as there were probably less than five Englishmen on the pitch, and anyway, now I had missed the ending and the adverts were on!

"You from London?" he persisted.

"No, I'm from the central part of England, the Midlands, North of Birmingham"

"Aah!" he nodded sagely, "Birmingham, Australia!"

Just then the Ticabus arrived and we embarked. You are allocated seats and the American was seated some rows behind me.

After a comfortable yet winding four-hour journey on the PanAmerican highway through the highlands of Central America with the coastal plain and blue Pacific Ocean down to our right, and green forested, white-cloud topped volcanos up to our left, we arrived at the border. All passengers had to debus to have their luggage searched and visas checked. Back on the bus and after less than half a mile we have to go through the same rigmarole again to enter Costa Rica.

As we finally set off for the leg to San Jose I turned and noticed that our American friend is no longer on the bus.

I asked a young woman who had been laughing and chatting with her friends, "Donde esta el hombre americano?" She shrugged and spoke quickly so I did not really understand, but I think she said something about a missing Costa Rican visa. But honestly I wasn't that bothered. He thought Australia had a Birmingham.

Costa Rica

I had expected Costa Rica to be full of life, but on the road it appeared just hot and dusty and empty, and we passed several volcanoes which used to be tourist attractions, but had suddenly become dormant. I got off at a small town called Upulua, where I had arranged a transfer to the hotel Cana Negra (black canyon). The hotel was open air with scattered cabanas in its gardens designed to attract wildlife. The gardens sloped down to an oxbow lake, with the Rio Frio just beyond. Suddenly there is life; beautiful birds, bountiful insects, butterflies and more. Outside my room, buzzing from flower to flower is a tiny electric blue humming bird. At the water's edge basked an 8-foot caiman which I inadvertently startled, and he splashed into the water, from where his eyes followed my every movement. Across to an island I spot the wonderfully named (and quite beautiful) Resplendent Roseate Spoonbill, and there are two horses up to high jinks. Well, he is. She is just trying to turn her flanks away, and kicking out when he gets too amorous.

Approaching dusk I dived into the forest behind the river and firstly followed a family of howler monkeys through the steamy canopy, then I foraged an equally steamy undergrowth to find a tiny Blue Jeans Poison Dart Frog, no bigger than my thumb nail. I'm not doing this alone; of course, I have Consuela, a daughter from the hotel to guide me. Tomorrow she is guiding me on the river. Finally, to herald the night I bathe in the swimming pool in the garden and watch the swallows dive and swoop one moment catching insects, the next scooping a drink from my pool. Drying off in the gathering gloom and making my way back to the cabana I spot lights in the grass. The lights are eye shine from my head torch, like tiny twin headlamps, and on closer examination I find that each are a set of eyes from myriad tiny wolf spiders that fill the lawn.

It is only one night since my scorpion experience and in the dark hours I am woken by a fearsome buzz in my left ear. I angrily wafted at it and it went away, but I spent the rest of the night under the sheet. The paranoia of the wee small hours soon took over and I became convinced I had been invaded by a parasitic wasp which had laid its eggs inside my head and had triumphantly buzzed off. My brain would now be slowly consumed by hatchlings, to be followed inexorably by a gradual but painful descent into madness. A little like supporting Walsall FC.

I'm up at dawn to join Consuela in her little outboard, and we chug along the Rio Frio spotting iguana in trees, caiman basking on banks and sandbars, and turtles lazing on rocks. The stars of the morning are kingfishers, darting in and out of the water from their low perches, and Consuela is quite excited at spotting all five of the indigenous species of Martin Pescador de Costa Rica; and of course there are herons, egrets, woodstorks, snakeb irds, trogons, hummin g birds, flycatchers and kiskadees galore.

We are joined on this mini-cruise safari by Peter. I had met Peter at dinner the previous evening, and he is a remarkable person, an example of whom everyone knows. Peter is a middle aged, slightly overweight, dour Scot, originally from Edinburgh, who has spent his working life as a low-ranking banker in institutions throughout ex-British colonies in Asia and Africa. His life with meaningless figures and among small minded ex-pats has given him a blinkered view of the world and has aided his inherent ineptitude; a little like a cross between Harry Worth and Mr McGoo. A perfect example of the eponymous Peter Principle, this Peter explained his philosophy in a softly spoken Edinburgh burr;

"Just keep your head down for forty years, don't screw the receptionist, and collect a nice pension," he smiled.

But this Peter, having lived a mollycoddled life without real responsibility epitomises clumsy ungainliness. This is the person all of those announcements about not forgetting personal belongings on buses and trains were invented for. He spills and drops everything, usually over other people; loses keys and spectacles and umbrellas, walks into things like trees and dog poop, gets lost, forgets where he is, and smiles at his own inadequate incompetency, constantly muttering "Ooh Dearrr!" to himself as if that atones for his clumsiness. Had he an ounce of self-awareness he would have given up on flight meals long ago, and the complications of sauce bottle, sachet, or carton access has always been a complete mystery to him. Totally oblivious to his own ineptitude, he has spent his whole life with people putting up with him. In the little while I had known him he had spilt tuna juice down Consuela's expensive dinner dress, ice cream down himself, and a glass of red wine (mine!) over the table. He had walked into a glass door marked pull, failed to access his hotel room because it involved turning a key and handle simultaneously, dropped his camera into the river, lost his sunglasses, and tried to tip us out of this little boat several times. Always accompanied by "Oooh Dearrr!", this is the disaster area known as Peter, and he is the last person you want to accompany you on a safari which necessitates silence, stealth and general awareness of the needs of not only fellow travellers, but also the animals, birds and insects you are trying not to disturb.

Consuela, to her eternal credit, was patience personified. I, on the other hand, would have swung for him had I had to spend one more day in his incompetent company.

I left Cana Negra after the river safari, and following lunch at an iguana restaurant at Muelle (they didn't serve iguana, but the premises were teeming with the huge wild lizards), I arrived at the Hacienda Pozo Azul to stay in a tent suite, advertised as "the ultimate ecoadventure stay where you sleep a canvas away from 4% of the world's biodiversity". Located in the heart of the Sarapiqui valley, I am sure the whole experience must be wonderful. However, when it rains constantly, one's judgement of any location tends to be negative. I have to admit I didn't enjoy my 24 hours in a tent suite. Firstly, I spent a fruitless hour trying to photograph two blue hummingbirds which were flitting from shrub to shrub (the futility of my farcical attempts would prove to be only two days from realisation), then on a nature trail through the forest, when I should have been curled up in bed and dry as every single creature of the forest proved to be, I forgot to change into proper footwear. The Crocs I had on for comfort when travelling proved to be worse than useless walking through the leaf litter. The holes for which their design is famous are perfect for letting in ants, and in this particular jungle, ants bite. Not only was it unbearably painful wearing them, the alternative proved far worse when flinging them off in desperation, as bare feet also pick up thorns and burrs and even more biting ants. I did however see two white-throated mannequin birds. These are the little warblers who invented the moonwalk long before Michael Jackson came along. I don't know which was funnier, their acrobatic displays, or me trying to photograph them whilst cursing and angrily hopping from foot to foot frantically trying to shake loose those wretched ants.

My final destination in Central America was the capital of Costa Rica, San Jose. Cool and nearly a mile high, nestled between volcanic ranges, it is a polluted and uninteresting sprawl, and I spent most of my time there organising on-going travel. But with one day to go I sign up for an excursion. Not my usual way of trying to see the sights, but I am tired and beginning to look forward to going home.

An early start on a coach full of tourists, first stop a coffee plantation, at least we get a cup of coffee. Then there are strawberries and wine tasting, maybe things are getting a little better. We spot a two toed sloth crawling along a telephone wire. Then we are up in the cloud forest and visiting the Poas

Volcano National Park. Everyone strolls to the main crater which unfortunately is full of cloud, next to one of the two crater lakes, Botos Lagoon which is similarly shrouded in mist.

The day could go either way. Maybe it is because my expectations are low that I am blown away by the sheer wonderfulness of the place we next visit, I would certainly elevate La Paz Waterfall Gardens to the top of anybody's bucket list.

It's not the aviary, beautiful as the parrots and toucans are, nor the butterfly conservatory, amazingly decorated as these huge insects flutter by, nor even the jungle cats; ocelot, margay, jaguarmundi, puma and jaguar, majestic, albeit a little sad in their captivity. It's not all these things, nor the frogs and monkeys and snakes and sloths. It is the hummingbird garden!

There are no nets or cages, just thoughtful flora and sugar-sweet feeders. It is the most magical place. It is humming bird heaven. There are 26 species of these tiny gifts from God which buzz past your ear, so close you feel the air from their wing beats. They perch and take in sustenance, then hover almost stationary so it appears, in the air sipping the nectar, then vanish as in an instant to reappear at the next feeder. Their wings are beating at an incredible hundred times a second. Their beauty is unsurpassed as they shimmer and sheen in metallic colours which flash in the sunlight. They have wonderful names like Violet Sabrewing or Scintillant Coppery Headdress. You can actually take feeders off the trees and the exquisite little creatures will come to you to feed. In my mind this is equal to swimming with dolphins or walking with gorillas or stalking with lions or any of those other wildlife experiences adventurers crave.

I sit and drink in the experience for a good hour, wander off to see the cats, then return, pop along to the aviary to let toucans perch on my head, then return, stroll into the conservatory and have six inch butterflies sit on my palm, then return. The 26 different hummingbirds they claim to have is the greatest concentration in the world. I love hummingbirds; I loved this place.

Finally, it is time to rejoin the tourist trail and make my way back to the coach. Leaving the gardens, you have to pass their five eponymous waterfalls; Las Cateratas; Templo, Magia Blanca, Encentada, Escondida and La Paz, each one worth the entrance fee. I tried the waterfall trick. Stare at the centre without blinking for 12 seconds, then look to the side; the ground rises!

I sleep back to San Jose, tomorrow the journey home begins in earnest.

Firstly, there is the late morning Ticabus to Managua, ten hours plus the usual border crossing farce; a fee for a stamp to leave one and a fee for a stamp to enter another. A friendly Salvadorean taxi driver helps me to the King Quality bus station where the security guard lets me sleep on three chairs to await the pre dawn departure. The King Quality bus is just that. Travelling through Nicaragua to El Salvador and Honduras, I am on the upper deck at the front in a fully reclinable seat with a 180-degree view. Where we stop, hot meals are brought aboard, and drinks are served all day. There are again the mind-numbing, time-wasting, ostensibly pointless border crossings, but the beds are comfortable, and the views divine!

We arrive 18 hours later in Guatemala City, too late for a hotel, but too early to check in at the airport. There are rumours New York is snowed in, but they prove unfounded. Eventually I board for Houston. Three hours in Houston and board for Newark, and six hours to Birmingham (England!). Then, you might expect , a short hop home on the local train. But believe it or not at the end of this wonderful odyssey, I am subjected to the extraordinary British institution that is the replacement bus service. It takes four hours, and the driver doesn't even know the route, I have to direct him to every station. Who knows what happened to the bus once I got off, but honestly I wasn't that bothered.

*

The Rainbow Tour
From Rio to the Big Apple

In my quest to discover the most magnificent waterfalls in the world, I am drawn to Iguazu Falls of which FLOTUS Eleanor Roosevelt once said "Poor Niagara!", meaning that in height, span, volume and sheer resplendence, Iguazu dwarfs Niagara, considered to be the most famous horseshoe falls on Earth. Carlucho and Gloria from Venezuela had also insisted these were the best.

Iguazu Falls are in the middle of South America, and form part of the border between Brazil, Paraguay and Argentina. Wondering how many birds I could kill with one stone in my planning, I find a tour which will take me from Rio De Janeiro, to Buenos Aires in seven nights. Allowing for overnight flights, that is perfect for half term. Eva Peron famously undertook a Rainbow tour of Europe. It didn't go well, the wife of an Argentine fascist touring post-war Europe, and she looked tired! Anyway, here I will be doing the return leg.

Rio De Janeiro, Day 1

Thus I found myself early one saturday morning on Copacabana beach ready to explore.

(There had been a slight hiccup when the Friday evening Birmingham flight into Paris was delayed by ice, and myself and four others were whisked off the flight and taxied to the direct Rio flight across the tarmac of Charles De Gaulle, in a Renault. A flight back in time, transfer to a business hotel just back from the beach, quickly drop off my bags and emerge at the confluence of Ipanema and Copacabana.)

I looked left and could see in the distance the unmistakable profile of Sugar Loaf Mountain, unfortunately sporting a cloudy hat. First I walked across an empty beach (it is only 8:30, after all), beautiful sand between my toes to the sea. The breakers which eventually came to a gentle lap on the shore, were from the Atlantic, and paddling in this water was like entering a warm bath.

Leaving the sea but remaining barefoot on the firm, wet sand, I headed north to the Sugar Loaf headland. Copacabana is a huge sweep of beach, and as I walked past the imposing art deco facade of the beautiful Copacabana Palace Hotel, I contemplated my situation. Yesterday afternoon I had been teaching in an ordinary Black Country school. Less than 24 hours later I am in a different hemisphere, a different continent, on the most famous beach in the world, walking towards the world's most famous iconically shaped mountain, in Brazil, the 5th largest country in the world (about to transfer to the 8th largest, Argentina), through which runs the majority of the Amazon river, the largest by volume, and the Amazonian rainforest which not only contains the most diverse flora and fauna of the world, but is also, dauntingly described as the lungs of the planet. I felt pretty insignificant, and rather honoured to be here.

At the end of the beach as it became a rocky promontory there was a small car park, and opposite a gateway into the Pao Azucao called the Trilha de Urca. I wasn't ready to go up the mountain itself, for which you need the cable car, as it was in cloud, so I decided to discover this trail. What a joy, and apparently a favourite for the Cariocas, Rio residents. As you begin the trail you are immediately in steaming forest and surrounded by butterflies, monkeys, lizards, leaf-cutting ants and the sound of myriad birds. There are huge spiders, stationary (thank goodness!) in their webs slung across the thick vegetation, and the monkeys are so playful, obviously used to being fed by ramblers. I can't tell if they are Capuchins, Marmosets or Tamarins, as they all look like the Mogwai from Gremlins. The trail follows the contour of the Morro da Urca and gradually climbs with the ocean constantly in view. After an hour I reached the top, which is the second level for the cable car. The next stretch, to the top of Sugarloaf first crosses a deep ravine before the precipitous ascent which currently disappears high into the mist. The air is clear enough at this level for me to turn and look east and savour my first sight of Christ the Redeemer (El Cristo Redentor) perched high on the peak of Corcovado Mountain, emerging above the clouds. It is supposed to loom over Rio, but from here looks very small indeed, a long way away. Below lies the white modern high rise buildings of the city, to my left and south, stretches the gentle curve of Copacabana beach along which I recently walked, and to my right and north are two more bays with beaches and gleaming white yachts moored everywhere; a millionaire's paradise. There is a helipad just below and copters are buzzing around no doubt giving tourists the bird's eye view. Corcovado, and Rio itself are surrounded by forested mountains.

Once I had descended it was time for lunch, and at the trail exit was a car with its boot open to reveal a small oven and gas hob. The very friendly couple cooking the street fare sold me a huge hot dog with onions and spicy relish for a couple of reals. I retraced my steps along a busier Copacabana beach back to my hotel where I slept till early evening, trying to disobey my body clock.

This time when I emerged I turned right onto Ipanema beach, this is where the beautiful people gather! It was crowded, standing room only, young people, socialising, chatting, in groups, posing, being there. What was also striking was how friendly everybody was. As a quite old (in this company) solo observer in hiking boots, khaki shorts, striped shirt and panama hat, I must have stuck out like a sore thumb, but everybody waved, smiled and greeted me as I walked past. I almost felt like royalty. Eventually it just got too much for me, I got rid of everything but the shorts and went and stood in the sea, and almost blended in.

It had been a long day, over 30 hours. So once it got dark I found a seat in a beach bar, drank beer, watched football being played on the TV and on the sand, and just chilled in a warm 24 degrees Celsius. Heaven!

Day 2

Not allowing myself to linger over breakfast, aware I had a bus leaving at 3pm, I took a minibus up to the Christ the Redeemer statue. As we climbed out of the city centre, the office blocks became smaller and dingier, as did the tenement homes. The higher we rose, the smaller and less well developed became the infrastructure until we reached the favelas, shanty town dwellings without mains facilities, but there are schools, bars, electricity cabling, water stand pipes, and satellite dishes attached to every home, however humble. The panoramic views back to the city and the ocean become more spectacular with each hairpin bend, until we stop and walk up to Him.

You approach the statue from the rear, seeing only its white robes and outstretched arms. Climbing the stairs, there is an altar, and a full Roman Catholic mass in progress, with all the pomp and ceremony you expect from it being performed at one of the church's most famous icons. Everyone from the altar boys to the priests are sporting golden vestments which gleam in the morning sunshine, and the orthodox and richly decorated Bishop's Mitre shines above all like a beacon.

I couldn't dally at the mass, I had to see the statue. I walked around the balustrade turned and looked up, and nothing prepares you for the majesty and simplicity and beauteous, peaceful countenance of the figure with outstretched arms in front of me. Pure white and shining in its magnificence, the Christ truly does look into your soul as it embraces the city. With a height of 125 feet, and span of 92 feet, the soapstone sculpture is as impressive as could ever be imagined, and as you walk away from it to the two levels of balcony, to perceive and gaze upon the 360-degree panorama over which He reigns it remains breath-taking from every angle. Vultures serenely glide above and below, ever watchful. There are monkeys, coatis, butterflies and birds, but the views; the ocean, the mountains, the city; the beaches I visited yesterday, the Maracana Stadium, and most importantly the Sugarloaf Mountain itself, no longer shrouded in mist, I had to set foot on its peak before I could leave.

The minibus took me back to the city where the streets are gridlocked, and then I taxied to the cable car. The first leg took me up to the Morro De Urca, very much a deja vu moment, but I could not dawdle, I had to summit, so immediately transferred to the next car. Up and up we passed over the mountain's flanks which appeared sheer and impossible to climb, and finally to the top, sublime. There was no cloud, the views were dramatic, especially back across to Corcovado. This is by now, panorama overkill, but simply to ensure my brain could be filled with Kodak moments I stayed for 40 minutes to savour and cement the achievement. This is Rio, one day I will return for something called Mardi Gras!

I was over an hour late for the bus station, but that was OK because the bus was over an hour late leaving. This was a five-hour journey south to Paraty. Ocean to my left, wooded mountains to my right, I was travelling the Costa Verde, but saw little of it as we had a moonless night.

Paraty, Day 3

Paraty is a historic colonial town with cobbled streets and full of beautifully painted stucco buildings. If this was the States, people would be walking around in 17th/18th century dress illustrating the living history. This is not the States. Everything is colourfully single storey except the churches which are whitewashed with high bell towers, and there are green spaces where horses graze and finches flock. It was a thriving port during the Brazilian gold rush, but now seeks to appease tourists on their way from Rio to Sao Paolo.

I had one day here, so after exploring its streets and buildings, I headed for the port and booked a ride out into the bay and around some of its outlying islands which included an excellent chicken lunch. The snorkelling in these green waters, made murkier by the overcast cloud, was good, if with no tropical reef. There was the customary jettisoning of the lunch left overs which prompted the usual feeding frenzy, amongst which when snorkelling, could be quite disconcerting. Especially when you wonder which larger fish might be attracted to the feast you could become a part of!

That evening after dinner I had a beer or two a with a lovely Australian couple, John and Maggie from Melbourne. I find folk from Melbourne very much more down to earth than any of their Sydney or Brisbane or even Perth neighbours. Maybe it is something to do with the weather, which is much more comparable to that in Britain. In the course of conversation John said that before he retired he had been working with the police and the coroner's office. "It's a bit difficult to describe," he admitted, "but you've seen CSI Miami? Well I would have been CSI Melbourne," he smiled, almost bashfully.

Foz, Day 4

It rained all the way to the airport at Sao Paolo, six hours, which appeared to be continually uphill through dense forest. Checked in at midday.

Brazil was colonised by the Portuguese, and became independent in 1822. History shows that the Portuguese tended not to expand by seizing land too far from the coast, see Goa, Sri Lanka, Macao; their influence overseas was not as all-encompassing as, for example, the British in India. Therefore, Brazil only has its language and football as a colonial legacy. Its people are ethnically diverse, as a result of African (forced) and European (voluntary) migration. They are a melting pot of people (see Blue Mink), with the majority of its 210 million population either white or Pardo, a term used to describe a mix of ethnic ancestries. The Sao Paolo metropolis with over 22 million people is now the largest city with the largest economy in the Southern Hemisphere. I was here simply to fly to Foz do Iguacu, an hour and a half.

I had my first view of the falls as we came into land. They looked just like a white gash in a huge green forest canopy, but at that height, looks can be deceiving. This is the state of Parana, and Foz is known as La Terra das Cataratas, land of the waterfalls. The Iguazu is a tributary of the Parana river which flows into the Atlantic via the River Plate, the widest river mouth in the world.

Straight out of the airport onto a bus, and reach the falls' visitor centre and gift shop in time to buy a poncho like the ones you have for the log flume at Alton Towers. This was a little more than a log flume, though. At nearly two miles wide, with 275 drops, the highest of which is 270 feet, and many hundred smaller ones, the Upper Iguazu cascades into the lower Iguazu. The largest is a long, narrow chasm called the Devil's Throat (La Garganta del Diablo), and there is an elevator from the visitor centre to a viewing platform at the top. It is a wonderful 180-degree vista of heavy cascades. I viewed the falls from both this elevated position, and several more viewing points, sometimes actually standing behind the huge wall of water. It was marvellous to see swifts flying in and out of the vertical water, and there were butterflies everywhere. The combination of humidity and spray made my skin a cocktail of saltwater soup, which attracted several butterflies to land on my hands and arms and feed accordingly.

There follows three hours of exploration after which I have to leave to go to Argentina. Before the border the bus driver delights in relating the irony that whilst most of the falls are in Argentina, Brazil has the best views. So I pass through border control at Puerto Iguazu and check into the hotel Alexander.

"Señor Leo He...He...Hayoffary?" attempts the clerk. " Es Ge...Ge, en Ingles. The He es un Ge, as in Geoffrey," I tried to help him. Hotels always assume Leo is my first name, so I never bother to try to correct them. But everyone has trouble with the gee sound, especially Spanish speakers.

"Ah, es Chayoffary, si?"

"Si, gracias. Buenas dias," I smiled.

"Buenos dias, Señor Chayoffary" he emphasised my name proudly having mastered it.

I located my room and went downstairs to enjoy a huge beer at poolside.

Argentina thinks itself above the rest of Latin America. Proverbially it is a Spanish speaking nation that thinks itself British but has an Italian disposition. I fell in love with Eva Duarte de Peron when I saw Joss Ackland as Juan Peron, David Essex, as Che, and Elaine Page as the eponymous heroine of Andrew Lloyd Weber and Tim Rice's pop opera, Evita. I had to see Buenos Aires, the Big Apple, and the Casa Rosada from whose balcony she spoke to her people, the descamisados (shirtless ones, or working class). This had been in June, 1978, in London's West End, well before the Falklands crisis, and nearly two decades before Maradona's Hand of God confirmed their reputation (among the English) as a nation of cheats. Eva had been an actress from a poor background who slept her way to the top, was despised by the middle classes, then confirmed her status as a goddess by dying young, in 1952, the year of my birth.

That evening I discovered three wonderful things about the Argentine. Everyone lives on steak, drinks the wine of the Malbec grape, an earthy, full bodied red, and dances the Tango, a sensual dance which is somehow stiff limbed, yet still ends up in a tangle of bodies. The steak was gorgeous, soaked in a garlic and herb butter, perfectly complemented by the Malbec and two marvellously supple dancers proudly showing off their moves with just a hint of swagger.

How many legends have a beautiful young girl escaping an unhappy marriage with a fresh faced, youthful lover? Well, that is how the falls were created. Naipi fleeing with Taroba in a canoe, when the enraged and cuckolded husband slices the river in two condemning the lovers to an eternity....in the Devil's throat, I suppose.

Puerto De Iguazu, Day 5

In the morning I notice a map of Argentina hanging on the wall behind the reception desk. Off the South East coast were two enlarged islands labelled Las Malvinas in large black letters. I think they think they belong to them!

After breakfast the people of Gran Aventura arrive to pick me up for a day of gallivanting. This begins with a truck safari through the secondary forest. "Why is it called secondary forest?" I enquired. "Because you can see the sky!" came the deadpan response.

I'm afraid the 30-minute safari was a little disappointing, all we saw were trees, and above the canopy, the sky. We stopped and descended 150 steps to a small pier where a boat awaited to take the group on a tour of the lower river. I was first off the bus, therefore first on the boat, and grabbed the front seat. True to form, the boat broke down hardly 100 yards into the trip and had to return to the pier and everyone de-boarded whilst another boat was brought into the dock. I was now first off the original boat, therefore last on the replacement boat. I managed to get an aisle seat amidships!

This was a rather fast speedboat which took us close and past many cascades before stopping in front of two large waterfalls. Slowly it edged forward into the water and everyone got a soaking. The force of the water hitting your head is incredible, like a jack hammer. It is impossible to upturn your head, the eyes and face couldn't take the pounding. The driver did this three times, before returning.

Being part of a group, I joined them for a walk of the Lower Route which brought us to a cafe for lunch as the heavens opened. With copious water still cascading from the sky we boarded a train to take us to the Upper Route and disembarked to walk across this fantastic river. The boardwalk seemed to take us for over a mile as the swollen river swirled menacingly just a few feet below. How they managed to build such a structure, I can only imagine there must be a dry season! Eventually we arrive at a viewpoint directly above the Devil's Throat, although a different Devil's Throat than I had experienced yesterday! Either way, Throat, Mouth or Cauldron, it illustrates the expansive nature of these falls that on either side there are many cascades, each one rivalling and indeed dwarfing other so-called world class sites. No wonder it has now achieved recognition as one of the Seven Modern Natural Wonders of the World.

It was indeed a wonder and a privilege to experience these waterfalls. We walked back to the train, cold and wet. The train took an age to deposit us at the bus, which took an eternity to drop me off at my hotel. I showered long to reintroduce warmth into my body. That evening the hotel was hosting a barbecue and dance at poolside.

Unfortunately, the rain cancelled the barbecue so I was directed with a number of other guests to a restaurant at the top of the hill outside the Alexander, where a beef roast was taking place. We entered a dark, smokey room and were seated at trestle tables. The smell of woodsmoke and fat was overwhelming, if not totally unlike the aroma of Sunday lunch at home. There was a huge fire with a cow being roasted on a spit and a very happy chef. He just couldn't stop laughing as he carved great slices of steak from immense curved ribs. The logs sizzled as splashes of fat hit them, the steam mixing with the smoke to make your eyes smart. I ordered a glass of wine and was brought a bottle of Malbec. A plate arrived with roasted meat and bread. There was a band playing, two guitarists, a drummer and a female singer, dressed like a

Spanish Flamenco dancer. They played and she sang more and more powerfully as the night wore on. She danced, people danced, even I was dancing. The chef continued to laugh as he beckoned us to take more meat. He would carve and expertly throw slivers of meat onto people's plates. I was now catching and devouring fillet steak as rare as rare could be. I finished my bottle of wine and asked for another glass, and was delivered another bottle. The band played on, people were joining in, singing, I was singing, although what songs I was caterwauling, I haven't a clue. Finally, I could take the merriment no longer and left. Outside the air was fresh and clear and I began to zigzag, very slowly, down the hill towards my hotel.

The next thing I know there is a knocking at my door and a disembodied voice pleading, "Señor Chayoffary, Señor Chayoffary. The taxi is here for the airport, you must hurry, Señor Chayoffary!". I'm on the bed, fully clothed, desperately trying to open my eyes and clear my head. I hadn't the foggiest as to how I'd got there, nor for that moment, where there even was.

Somehow I packed, washed, checked out and made it to the airport; checked in and discovered there was a two-hour delay for my flight. Time to source some breakfast.

Eva sang that Buenas Aires should stand back and understand what it would find in her. In the case of me, it was just a bit of hungover Chayoffary!"

Buenos Aires, Day 6

On the outskirts of any Central or South American city are the shanty towns; Favellas. But not Buenos Aires. There were several makeshift homes situated under flyovers, but nothing on the scale of Caracas, Lima or Rio. Two-hour delay, two-hour flight, transfer to hotel, and the day is almost gone. I had one place I needed to see, the Casa Rosada, literally the Pink House, this is where Eva preached to the throngs that crowded the Plaza de Mayo. Two blocks back from my hotel was the Avenida de Mayo, and a short walk along this and it opened onto the Plaza, mostly green with benches and statuary, and at the opposite end was the three storey rose building I had come to see. It is an Italianate Art Deco building, with a wide facade topped by several domes, slate roofs and ornate windows. In the centre it is raised with an Argentine flag and open arches. But I just sat and stared at the central balconies from where she had lit up the faces of the poor of Argentina, promising a brighter future, little knowing that hers was limited. "Don't Cry for Me, Argentina", Julie Covington, Elaine Page or Madonna. For me it shall always be Elaine.

I left and walked back along the Avenida Rivadavia for a dozen or so blocks until I came upon the famous Las Violetas. It is everything Argentina and its capital is famous for; false European Belle Epoque, the pre-war Golden Age of pomp and snobbery. The domain of the aristocracy who so railed against Eva's rise from being one of their illegitimate children to almost the Vice-Presidency. (They called her a whore! I can understand their mistake, I am still called a teacher, yet I have been retired some years). That said, the interior is a very pleasant regency style, the atmosphere a quiet murmur with the occasional chink of glass or china teacup, and I am sure the produce is of a quality with prices to match. It is just not my sort of club. When asking for a tip, I advised the waiter not to spill the red wine!

Day 7

It is strange how a tour can lose its edge once the main objectives are behind you. Rio with Sugarloaf, the beaches and La Corcovado, and Iguazo and the Casa Rosada have been ticked off (I hate that term, it consigns great places and the most marvellous experiences to a to-do list). I have one more objective then 24 hours to wait for my flight home.

It is not morbid to visit a cemetery, especially in a Latin Roman Catholic country. La Recoleta is one of the best, certainly up there with Parisian Pere Lachaise, if not as famous to contain the likes of Jim Morrison and Oscar Wilde.

The tombs, or mausoleums of La Recoleta are beautifully sculptured, mostly white marble with gothic, ornate architecture and holy or significant statuary, angels, lions, eagles, disciples, the virgin, the dead themselves. The tomb of Eva Peron is fairly simple in comparison to others in the cemetery. She is laid to rest in her family Duarte's tomb, but her embalmed body within the tomb is heavily fortified lest she go missing again as she did for 16 years from 1955. Her myth is so strong it is feared factions could use her to manifest uprisings. Argentinian politics have rarely held any stability, and Eva's immortality will always be a threat. Her tomb does indeed bear her words " No me llores perdida ni lejana..." Don't cry for me being lost and distant.

After a morning spent wandering the maudlin streets of La Recoleta I yearned to return to the living, and spent the rest of the day visiting the Japanese garden, with the usual water features and carp pools, and the botanical gardens, both remarkably beautiful places to spend quality time. I returned to the hotel via the Avenue of the 2nd July, the widest avenue in the world, then finished the day with a walk around the Puerto Madero admiring the yachts of the rich, and gazing across the mouth of the River Plate, the widest in the world to where Uruguay's capital, Montevideo must lie, 140 miles away.

I made the mistake of booking a tango lesson combined with a tango show and steak (again) dinner for my final evening. I was as successful dancing the tango as I had previously been learning the salsa in Cuba; I always end up doing some sort of twist. The whole thing was very touristy, something I generally try to avoid.

Clambering back on the bus after this night of dancing I found myself behind a young lady with a rather large backside, and wearing tight, light blue shorts. Well, you try not to look, as she climbed aboard, and I followed, but a little too quickly, and she suddenly stopped and stepped back crushing my nose.

"I'm sorry, I wasn't looking," I said, as my eyes watered. Very British.

La Boca, Day 8

I'm in my third day in Buenos Aires, nowhere can contain my attention for this long, so I am struggling to keep occupied. My flight home is late this afternoon so I take a bus to La Boca, a barrio in the South East of the city which is famous for the Boca Juniors football club. They play at the intimidating Bombanera stadium, steepling stands form a tight box around the pitch making acoustics to strike fear into opponents, and the area is steeped in history.

I found myself on El Caminito, the main strip full of brilliantly coloured clapperboard buildings of all shapes, sizes and hues; red, orange, yellow, blue, green. Most have balconies on which stand mannequins of gauchos, tango dancers, or Diego Maradona. At street level there are artists painting portraits, artisans selling local wares, women wrapping and frying empanadas, children with llamas, monkeys, iguanas or armadillos looking to make a peso for a photo, and bands of drummers thumping out a latin beat. Each cafe has musicians vying for attention as dancers whirl around. The atmosphere is lively, bright, friendly, heady and South American.

The history of La Boca is of welcoming poor European (mainly Italian) immigrants of the late nineteenth and early twentieth century. The houses were traditionally painted with leftovers from the ships that docked locally, and became brothels, bars and cheap, overcrowded lodgings as is the custom for refugee sanctuaries. From these rather sordid, disease-ridden, poverty stricken beginnings had evolved this gaudy, noisy, cosmopolitan tourist attraction.

I wandered the streets, albeit not too far from Caminito, the back streets have a reputation, they still contain her descamisados. Then I sat outside a bar, with a beer, in the sunshine watching the world tango by.

Above me was a balcony bearing life-sized statues of of Agustin Magaldi, Maradona and Eva in her best speech making pose. Across the street sat Paco on a wall, surrounded by six well-behaved dogs, ranging from a chihuahua to a rough collie. Paco wore cut-off jeans and nothing else. His small but perfectly proportioned bronzed body glistened in the sunshine, his long wavy hair not unlike that of the collie.

"Para las señoras de la Boca, I exercise their pooches," he explained.

"Ah, los perros?" I tried to confirm.

"Si, and sometimes their pussies," he grinned.

"Los gatos?" I interjected again.

"Oh no!" he confirmed with a laugh. "Pussies!"

My rainbow tour was ending, time for another suitcase in another hall. The whole experience had been surprisingly good for me.

Eleven hours to Paris, short hop to Birmingham, and train home. I'll be walking up my drive sometime tomorrow afternoon.

*

Chasing the Sunset:
Cuba to DR

Cuba played a huge role in my childhood. No-one knew where it was, only somewhere in Uncle Sam's back yard. Jamaica and Barbados were in the magical Caribbean, Cuba wasn't! It was just a place which had nearly caused the nuclear destruction of the planet. And because of the Cuban Missile Crisis, everyone was aware of four minute warnings, mushroom clouds and whitewashing the windows to reflect the heat of a nuclear blast. Thanks to Raymond Briggs' "When The Wind Blows", which came 20 years later, we also knew about radiation sickness, and the bleak prospect of a nuclear winter.

Being a Baby Boomer, or as I like to describe now, of the Call the Midwife generation, I lived through the Cuban Revolution, the catastrophic Bay of Pigs invasion, the Soviet Missile emplacements, Krushchev's shoe banging episode at the UN, and the assassination of John F Kennedy. Everyone knows where they were when they heard of the president's death, I was watching Emergency Ward Ten when the newsflash came on.

Fidel Castro was the skilled revolutionary who led the coup to rid Cuba of the authoritarian Fulgencio Batista, a president who was in the pocket of the Mafia and the American Government. Prior to Castro, Cuba was the sex, drugs and gambling playground of corrupt America. Once Fidel had given powerful offices to his brother Raoul, and their friend and close ally, the Argentinian doctor, Che Guevara, they kicked out the Mafia and set about nationalising foreign owned businesses. The USA claimed he was the puppet of Soviet Communism, and in response to missile emplacements, they blockaded the island. After tense negotiations during which World War Three was expected, the Soviets withdrew. The free world breathed again and turned its back on Cuba which became a virtual recluse until the end of the 20th century.

Cuban welfare turned challenging with the dissolution of the Soviet regime in the 1990's. Castro called this time 'the Special Period', and he was dubbed 'the Air Hostess' for imploring his people to tighten their belts. With their USSR coalition gone, the country headed a group of countries known as Non-Aligned, and became close to Chavez's Venezuela. The country gradually opened up and Canada and the EU and China became more involved. The US remained aloof and continued to shun Castro's regime. There were many conspiracy theories surrounding JFK's demise and attempts on Fidel. But they couldn't ignore their close neighbour forever, and with the handing of the reigns to Fidel's brother Raoul, a thawing of relations was on the cards.

In the early 21st century the call came to see Cuba now, before the Americans could return. I flew to Havana in early Spring, via Madrid. It was a flight during which I was always chasing the sunset.

I struck up a conversation with a young French nun (to be precise, she did with me), and during a lull we both stared out of the window at the sastrugi cloudscape which was slate grey, edged with a vivid red and yellow horizon. Suddenly she pointed "Voila! La Création!" she cried excitedly. I almost spilled my red wine.

Havana

Cuba is a very nervous country and it took over three hours to clear customs. I arrived at the Kohli hotel just in time for a drink, a bite to eat and bed. My body clock, as usual defeating me.

I had two days in Havana so set about discovering straight after breakfast, first stop the Necropolis de Christobal Colon, or as we would say, the Christopher Columbus City of the Dead. Many impressive mausoleums here, but I wanted to see the simple grave of La Milagrosa, the Miracle Worker known simply as Amelia.

She died in chidbirth aged just 23 in 1901, and was buried with her stillborn child at her feet. The Necropolis is so popular, bodies have to be exhumed after some years to put the bones in a box to free up room. When Amelia was exhumed, her body had not decayed, and her baby was in her arms. She has become the unofficial patron saint for those with special needs, especially childless couples, ever since.

Onto Revolution Square, the size of Tiananmen, and the place people gathered to be whipped up into a revolting frenzy by the Castro's. Today, strangely empty and overgrown with weeds; Che Guevara's image overlooking all, with his mantra "Our every action is a cry against imperialism".

Guevara became Castro's Foreign Minister and travelled the world educating the working classes in their struggle against despotism. He was captured in Bolivia by CIA trained forces in 1967 and shot dead without trial when he was probably worth more to his captors alive than dead. His execution ensured his immortality, and his image has featured on every socialist's tee shirt ever since.

Havana occupies a position in the west of centre, on the north coast of the island. The Island is 780 miles wide, yet only 119 miles wide at its widest point. On the shoreline is a wall and promenade, the Malecon, of which every Cuban is proud, and on which Habaneros can be seen walking, every evening.

You will recall "the hottest spot north of Havana" is the Copacabana night club in New York. Here at the entrance to the port there is a fort and lighthouse and grassy knolls around which I strolled after lunch, before walking the Malecon; five miles of looking out to sea. Occasionally there are little market places selling objets d'art and trinkets, illustrating how the economy is now open to little enterprises. It is amazing how we take so much for granted.

The food is simple. I dined on scrawny chicken with rice and beans and bread. The rice is spiced and tasty, but the bread crumbles into dry mounds of sawdust.

The next day I had to contend with torrential rain. I opted for indoor sightseeing, however the cathedral was closed, so after circling the flea market and feeling sorry for the dripping wet stall holders, I found the Museo de la Revolution which depicted the glorious struggle against the murderous, imperialistic, tyrannical pigs. There were impressive guerrilla warfare tableaux with waxworks of our heroes. I hope I am not belittling their worthy efforts when I admit to being reminded of Robert Lindsay's Wolfie Smith and his Power to the People cry for the Tooting Popular Front.

Unable to contend further with the rain I found El Floridita, an old haunt of Ernest Hemingway. His statue leans on the corner of the bar. I spent the afternoon drinking beer and being serenaded with all sorts of latin rhythms by the most wonderful band. In between samba and merengue I got talking to two medical students, Bruno and Sylvia, who told me how the system works,

The average or common wage is about 15 CUC's a month, around £10, but there is a lower value peso which they also use. The state provides simple rations of rice and beans and other staples for every citizen, but these are for subsistence and only last about ten days, after which you have to live on what you can make in farmer's markets or on the back market. Many families try to keep grandparents "alive" to continue to claim their rations, but there are inspectors who check everything. If a horse, ox or goat dies, they will replace it, but not abuela.

Cuba's greatest export, even beyond cigars, is the medical profession. There are Cuban doctors and nurses operating throughout the world creating foreign currency income for the state.

Only now are people realising that communism has held the country back. The ideology that the state will plan and provide, that all wealth will be divided, that all people are equal; has worked against invention, enterprise, ambition, and therefore progress and growth. A Cuba stuck in the 1960's is now embracing the 21st century.

I bade goodnight to my doctor friends and returned to the hotel tipsy yet chastened from my lesson. I was surprised to find a professional troupe performing an aqua ballet of Carmen in and around the hotel pool. Surreal!

Cuba is famous for many things. The largest island in the Caribbean, with the oldest Latin American railway. Some marvellous amateur athletes like the heavyweight boxer and triple Olympic gold medallist, Teofilo Stevenson, and Alberto Juantorena, the double Olympic gold medallist runner, of whom David Coleman famously observed that down the back straight "...the big Cuban opened his legs and showed his class".

Ironically, Cuba is famous for its cigars which sell for a premium all over the world. Every town you visit you are invited into factories to witness their production and buy some. Young men beckon you into their family homes, typically one room in a tenement block, to buy a black market box. They are apocryphally rolled on the thighs of nubile virgins, although what that's supposed to do to the taste I can only imagine. Talking about taste, the smoker can only taste smoke, those around are invaded by an interesting aroma, which once stale just stinks, and if you take them down as Selma and Patti, Marge Simpson's twin sisters once remarked, in suitably gravelly voices, "It's like smoking twenty fags at one time!" The market, thankfully for all cancer inducing sticks, is shrinking.

Be that as it may, the Cuban authorities are very jealous of this industry and will prosecute those seeking to smuggle boxes out of the country. On leaving Cuba I was asked to accompany customs officials to a basement room for a random search. This was very tense and I worried should any officer be seen to don rubber gloves. I had one box of cigars I had bought for "personal use", and thankfully I was allowed to continue my journey. However, the guy next to me had a suitcase full of Romeo y Julietas, perhaps 36 boxes each containing 25 cigars. His case was confiscated and he was carted off to the cells.

But Cuba is most famous for its motor cars. These are classic American models from the 1950's, frozen in time with the blockade and then the continuing cold war. And they still exist, cruising the Malecon, posing in car parks, taxiing tourists. The most brightly gleaming models work in Havana and the tourist resorts, but original Pontiacs, T/birds and Bel Airs, can still be seen, rather beat up, but lovingly cared for in the backwaters.

There are some 60,000 on the island, Cadillacs, Chevy's, Dodges, Buicks and Fords, seemingly fresh off the Detroit production line over 60 years ago. In reality this does seem impossible, and when you investigate these cars, the engines don't sound the same, the bodywork glows too brightly, the leather seats lack wear and tear. Someone, somewhere (actually there are probably many small and large enterprises) is pimping these old cars up; new wings here, replacement Korean engines there, speciality white wall tyres, and so on. Cuban cars, which contribute millions of tourist dollars (metaphorically) are more likely to resemble Trigger's broom:

totally original, just had 17 new heads and 14 handles.

"Look after your broom" Trigger says enigmatically.

"And your broom will look after you?" Rodney suggests.

"No, Dave. Just look after your broom."

West to Maria La Gorda

I left Havana, west for Las Terrazzas, a 30 year-old eco experiment in the Sierra Del Rosario mountains, where old coffee plantations are being allowed to return to rainforest. The resulting biosphere is rich in flora and fauna, and includes lush hillsides, lakes, rivers and waterfalls, and some of the longest zip wires in the world.

The one-hour journey took me out on 5th Avenue, past impressive haciendas now housing embassies and the offices of multi-nationals. Once in the countryside you could see farmers' fields being worked with oxen, and poor villages which always had a schoolroom located next to the soldiers' barracks. In one village I saw soldiers playing on the children's swings and slides.

On arrival at a small farmhouse I took a two-hour trek into the forest looking for birds, but succeeded in seeing many butterflies and the ever present turkey vultures. At one junction, trying to be helpful, I picked up a piece of litter intending to dispose of it properly at the first opportunity. Unfortunately, I had disturbed a host of green ants who were evidently feeding happily on the sweet contents. They immediately directed their fierce mandibles and stinging abdomens to my own innocent hand and arm, and yelling painfully, I was forced to discard the litter guiltily back into the undergrowth. Many of the ants remained on their new host, and I remained uncomfortably in pain until able to wash back at the farmhouse.

A group of us dined wonderfully on homemade chicken and rice and beans. The farmer, his wife and sons serenaded us with Cuban folk tunes whilst our lunch's relatives wandered around our feet, pooing in revenge.

I checked in at La Moka hotel, built in and around the forest, a huge banyan tree grows through the lobby, my room felt it was more outdoors than in, an interesting and clever effect. There was a guided trail down to the waterfalls of San Juan, and it was a very pleasant 40-minute jaunt. I played in the warm waters sliding down various little chutes, then dozed in the sunshine watching the clouds, butterflies and TV's. As the latter circled lower and began to roost in the canopy I guessed it was time to return and I regained my room by dusk.

Dinner is notoriously boring in eco hotels, and La Moka didn't disappoint. No music, no entertainment, just bland vegetarian fare served by earnest but well-meaning waiters. A very solemn affair helped to its conclusion, thank goodness, with cold bottle so beer..

There are three canyon zips from La Moka, all good adrenalin fuelled rides. Number one takes you down from the hotel to the village, then walk up to the second which is a 400-yard trip across the lake, constant stunning views, if you can concentrate on them. Finally, a 300-yard zip across the lower lake and bridge to the exit, although I had to climb back up to the hotel for my bags.

I'd zipped after breakfast and spent the rest of the day walking in the Soroa hills before taking a bus to Viñales. Here I satyed at the Aguas Cuvas camp, in a chalet. It reminded me of the summer camp from Dirty Dancing, and when they tried to teach guests the Samba, I deliberately sat myself in the corner. In the evening a few guests were invited to a Panedor. This is purportedly an illegal home restaurant. I suppose people aren't allowed to use their homes for black market operations.

Four of us were met in reception by a young man who packed us into his small car, drove into the town centre and dropped us off at a petrol station. Looking very furtive he then walked us to a small house where we were greeted by the Señora. She led us into her front room and fed us a strange fish meal whilst we sat around the walls, cross legged. The furtive youth then took us back to the camp for more dancing. Very strange.

Next day, I went on a hike around the Mogates of Viñales valley. These are limestone walls and outcrops from ancient collapsed caverns. Sometimes the cavern still exists, and these were included on the walk. I lunched at a farmhouse where I learned of their ancient agricultural practices and more of how the communist system operates. Up to 60 corrupt inspectors examining every aspect of work and life to validate meagre rations and keep the peasants in the dark ages; idyllic and suppressed.

In the late afternoon I took the bus to Maria La Gorda, the western most point of Cuba. The further west we go the poorer the roads and the communities, and I am still chasing the sunset. During the drive I was talking to Susan, a teacher from Prince Edward Island, about Chitty Chitty Bang Bang. Why totally escapes me, except I had always rankled that here was an English story about an English family's adventures in a magical English car, written by the English Ian Fleming, yet the song from the film calls the car "Our fine, four-fendered friend"! This is a clear Americanism for the wings of a car. We discussed more Americanisms; hood for bonnet, trunk for boot, fawcett for tap, pants for trousers, purse for handbag, and we realised that the list is almost endless. We recalled over a hundred between us, ending with their inability to pronounce words like mirror, lieutenant, and aluminium. "You do the math" she laughed, as I bristled. Still, it passed the journey. The last hour in the pitch black on a potholed dirt track was extremely uncomfortable as you didn't know when the next lurch would hit. That last 20 miles we saw no hint of a village or homestead. That is how isolated this little piece of heaven is.

It was well after dark when we arrived at the Villa Maria La Gorda (Fat Mary's House), and I had time only to see the beach under the stars. Gazing out to sea, across the Caribbean I knew that the next landfall was Mexico's Yucutan peninsular.

In daylight the beach had soft white sand, was palm fringed and the sea was calm, warm and blue. The idyllic Caribbean beach scene. And it was empty. I had my mask and snorkel and swam out about 400 yards looking for coral, but there was very little, a few encrusted rocks with small sergeant majors, fusiliers and a few wrasses, quite disappointing. Then as I headed for shore I found three false jetties which had been deliberately sunk to attract coral growth. The shoals of fish surrounding these were much more impressive. Finally, at the shoreline, the real jetty, a much older affair was absolutely festooned with coral and fish. There were butterflies, angels, groupers, triggers, surgeons, damsels and dominoes, puffers, pipes and cornets. Away from the piles were anemones with clown fish, and on the sandy sea bed, colourful rays and eels. At the eyeline, on the surface, menaced barracuda. Cleaner wrasses busied themselves and the odd giant trevally occasionally solemnly swam by. Swimming in and out of the ancient piles was like diving a wreck. It was the perfect place to hone one's snorkelling skills, and I happily spent the whole day swimming, sunbathing, and once the sun had sunk below the yardarm, drinking. Dined on red snapper to end the perfect day.

The Dominican Republic

My adventures in Cuba were now at an end, and I headed back to Havana. Whilst I had been gallivanting around this corner of the Caribbean my good lady had been soaking up the sun in a stylish hotel on the north coast of the DR. I flew to Puerto Plata (after a brief dalliance in customs) to join her as we had one very particular adventure we had planned to do together.

The island of Hispaniola, east of Cuba is one of those few islands of the world which are split into different countries (Great Britain is another), and one of only two in the Caribbean.

The western half is French speaking Haiti, one of the poorest countries in the world famous for having the misfortune to be ruled by the wicked "Papa Doc" Duvalier, in the 1960's. Extremely cruel and highly superstitious, Papa Doc invoked the ancient mysticism of Voodou to rid himself of enemies. His secret police, called the Tonton Macoute, were little more than an undercover death squad, and there are stories of Papa Doc witnessing many of their most wicked torture techniques. He once thought an enemy had transformed himself into a black dog, and ordered the killing of all black dogs in the country. Haiti had the double misfortune to have his son, Baby Doc succeed him. The country still suffers from poverty, and unfortunately seems to take the brunt of the Caribbean's fiercest hurricanes, and even earthquakes.

Spanish speaking Dominican Republic, or the DR, is not untarnished itself. In the 1930's its US backed president Rafael Trujillo had over 30,000 Haitian migrants massacred by machete to remove any evidence (rifles and bullets) of army involvement. Since he himself was assassinated, 30 years later, the country has grown in wealth, helped in the main by America's desperation to keep the communists out. Today it is a relatively peaceful country enjoying the largest economy in the Caribbean and Central American region.

I met up with Kaz at the Bachata Hotel, west of Puerto Plata, on Maimon Bay and over dinner she told me a disconcerting story.

The Baie de Maimon has long been a protected area because of its diverse marine life and surrounding forests, but recently a cruise terminal had been built called Amber Cove. This is an exciting development, as the port will bring in cruise ships and tourists (especially American) by the thousand; many dollars to be made. Sadly, for the residents and shop keepers of the area, these tourists are all herded onto coaches and taken into Puerto Plata to take the cable car up Mount Isabella and see the replica of Christ the Redeemer, or to visit Ocean World to swim with dolphins.

In creating Amber Cove a large area of the seabed had to be dynamited to make a deep water approach. The effect of this has been to kill the coral for miles around. This has not only decimated the marine life, but also made the beaches dangerous. The beaches are advertised by the tour operators as being a beautiful playground for families and their children, with warm waters and clean, white sand gently sloping into the sea. They have neglected to mention the pieces of razor sharp coral which wash up daily and have caused no end of lacerations to people (especially children) whose only mistake was wanting to paddle or play in the surf. The likes of the Carnival Cruise Line and TUI (Thomson's) deny liability as they claim the beaches belong to the government. They refuse to take any responsibility for their false advertising claims.

Putting this sad state of affairs behind us we prepared for our adventure.

A taxi picked us up at dawn to take us on the four-hour journey to Semana Bay. Bobby was very good, knowing where we were going he gave Kaz two seasickness tablets. "You will need them, best take them now" he reassured.

It was an easy way to see the country, a single carriageway road took us through Puerto Plata, past other resorts like Sosua and Calabrete, along the coast to Nagua where we stopped for breakfast and to stretch our legs. We arrived at Santa Barbara de Samana at 10 am and were immediately met by Ricardo, the captain of the catamaran which would take us into the bay. We soon realised that many boats leave the jetty at this time, and every boat has one objective, to find the humpback whales.

Samana Bay on the North East coast is an east facing inlet and mating and birthing ground for humpback whales. There are strict rules for watching the whales, should you be lucky enough to come across one, you should spend no more than five minutes at a respectful distance, observing, and not harassing the creature. They are here in the Springtime, to mate, then return one year later to give birth and suckle and prepare for wherever they go next. Many believe they are on a continuing round trip to Antarctica.

All of the boats are in radio contact, or used to be, these days it is simpler to stay in touch by phone. It is a little like hunting leopard, you don't have to look for the cats, just the Toyota cruisers which have spotted them first.

I instructed Kaz, "Don't worry about photos or videos, just drink in what you see, don't do it through a lens." As it happened, she videoed the whole trip.

It was just wonderful being on the water, bobbing up and down, seeing the wooded slopes on three sides, the bay is reputed to be one of the most picturesque in the world.

After an hour or so, we were well into the middle of the bay and straining our eyes for tell tale signs; breaching, flippers, water spouts; desperate to be able to shout "Thar she blows!". Ultimately, and almost anti-climatically Ricardo drew alongside a mother and calf. By the size of her back and dorsal fin, she was much larger than the 33 foot boat, but she calmly swam, occasionally surfacing to breath, alongside us, with her calf, sometimes behind, sometimes parallel. We never saw her head, although I thought I caught her eye, and only glimpsed her forward flippers, which were white, and didn't see her flukes. The same with the baby. But we spent about 10 minutes with them, always at a respectful distance, never hassling them, just, peacefully sharing a moment or two with these wonderful leviathans of the ocean. Sometimes they would be port side, and sometimes to the starboard, but after a little while Captain Ricardo turned the boat away, looked at us and said "Lunch?"

We could only nod, still in awe.

Ricardo dropped us off at the Cayo Levantado, a small island opposite Samana town. Sunbathing and swimming here was gorgeous, even if we had to dodge the showers we could see coming in from the east, and we took lunch at a beachside restaurant, the fare much improved from Cuba.

Bobby was waiting at the harbour side when we eventually

returned, "Did you see the whales?" he asked, and we nodded, still in awe. We dozed as Bobby drove us back, always in forest, occasionally the canopy opened up to reveal the ocean to our right. It was soon dark, and I noticed a large moon had risen over the ocean. Tomorrow is the full moon, I thought.

After a hotel buffet breakfast and following Kaz's revelations I decided to check out the bay. I snorkelled and quickly discovered the water throughout was murky, almost greasy, and there was no life, save for a few sea urchins. As I left the water a wave broke and I felt something hit my leg. I didn't realise until I was drying off that I was bleeding from a cut to my ankle. Steel sharp slivers of shrapnel were being churned up with every wave. Looking along the beach there was not one parent allowing their child to play in the sea.

It was our last day and Kaz relaxed around the pool while I discovered a lagoon full of terrapins and catfish, and mangroves loaded with roosting egrets and yellow weaver birds at the rear of the hotel.

To catch the sunset we walked up to a promontory with an attractive white pagoda evidently used for bride and groom photography. We were not the only ones with this idea, there were several people before us, some picnicking, one couple toasting each other with champagne, everyone facing west as the sun sank slowly behind the distant shore. It was a breathtaking sunset, and as people were leaving I suddenly remembered the full moon, and about turned to see it rising above the horizon. No-one was looking east until I exclaimed and pointed. The first time I had seen this phenomenon; synchronised sunset and moonrise. A perfect end to this dual island adventure.

At the airport, re-connecting with the world, I heard the news of the untimely death of André Previn, the academy award winning composer and conductor of the London Symphony orchestra, among others. He was equally famous for being the star of a Morecambe and Wise sketch where Eric was playing Grieg's Piano Concerto, badly.

"You are playing all the wrong notes", laments Previn.

Eric rises from the piano, grabs him by the lapels, grits his teeth and says, "I think you'll find I was playing all the right notes, but not necessarily in the right order."

Cue guffaws of laughter and Mr Andrew Preview's induction into the Pantheon of British Comedy.

I recalled teaching a class of 16 year-olds how to construct their C.V.s Coming alongside Sophie Smith tapping away at her keyboard, I note that both her spelling and sentence construction leave a lot to be desired. Almost every word is misspelt, as in "i wud of bin a heir dreser but now im trainin in nales and beouty"

"Sophie, you'll need to improve your spelling, or you'll have difficulty getting any interviews", and I sat with her a while trying to help her untangle her efforts.

The next day I received a visitor, Mrs Smith, "What you mean tellin' our Soaf she'll never gerra job?", she was rather angry. I tried to explain that's not what I said, but she was in no mood to listen. "I'll 'ave you know she's won awards for 'er typin'. She can do a farsand characters a minute."

"I understand that, Mrs Smith," I said, and seized my chance, "but are they all necessarily in the right order?"

I'm afraid it fell on stony ground, but in my mind's eye Sophie became a marine biologist.

*

The Lost City Of Teyuna

I was asked if I'd visited the Lost City. And therein lies the conundrum; how can you have a known lost city? If it used to be lost but now is found, then it can no longer be a lost city. It can be a rediscovered city, an abandoned city, a ruined city, or even just a city, in as much as being as it used to be a city, then a lot of people had once founded and lived in it. If it remains lost, then it has yet to be discovered. It is a little like the tomb of Tutankhamun; Egyptologists believed there might be an undiscovered royal tomb in the Valley of the Kings, but didn't know where it was nor to whom it belonged (certainly not the British Museum, at least!). That could be called the Lost Tomb, until, of course it had been found. Similarly, the world assumes that Christopher Columbus in his search for a western passage to India discovered the Americas, as if those lands were uninhabited. The truth of course is that Columbus invaded the Americas for the Europeans; they had always been inhabited by Native Americans, and weren't even lost.

In many cases, Lost Cities, especially in the Americas, became lost cities because they were abandoned before the

Europeans could "find" them and pillage, plunder, sack them and claim them for their own. Machu Picchu is a case in point, as is Teyuna, the city of the four tribes of Tairuna. To them it is not a lost city, just one abandoned by their forefathers at the height of the Spanish Conquest and subsequently robbed of its gold by a series of undisciplined adventurers.

I like to think of myself as a disciplined adventurer who wouldn't dream of taking anything but photos and leaving nothing but footprints. And so it was that, armed with these principles, a sleeping bag and a decent set of walking boots that I boarded three planes, from Birmingham to Madrid, on to Bogota, and culminating in Cartagena, one of the most amazing cities I have ever had the pleasure to party in, on my way to hiking up to La Cuidad Perdida. There, it sounds much better in Spanish.

Colombia receives a bad press. There's the civil war between the government and the FARC, the battle against the powerful drug barons, and of course drug smuggling and all its attendant ills. In fact, as soon as I declared I was to visit the country, I began to get advice from all corners, not least the tongue-in-cheek comments about making sure I packed my own bags and remained vigilant to offers of alleged talcum powder.

The truth, as I was to learn, was vastly different. Thanks to intelligent use of Agent Orange, the illegal Coca plantations had been eradicated. This had taken the power away from the drug barons, which now toothless, had been easy meat for the law enforcers. An enlightened government had all but made peace with the revolutionaries who ultimately had little to revolt about, and all the spare land and labour force had now been put to work creating the world's second biggest exporter of flowers.

In fact, it was my visit to Colombia which began to open my eyes to the constant bad news propaganda we are fed from the BBC which only appears to want to peddle the negative aspects of countries around the world, especially in the so-called third world. Subsequent travels around the world have confirmed those suspicions, especially in regards to the fomentation of the Arab Spring. Alas, I don't want to get political, these are just my untrained observations. (During the last recession and worldwide financial crisis, the BBC seemed to delight in talking down the UK economy, always highlighting bad news, not the good. To this end they constantly depicted a graph behind the newsreader with a doommongering downward curve and arrow)

Cartagena

I landed in Cartagena having organised accommodation in the old town at Hostal Casa Mamallena, and they were sending a car for me, price $15. However, I had managed to get an earlier connection from Bogota, and although I had emailed ahead, there was no car waiting for me at the airport.

I approached a taxi. No, that is wrong, I am surrounded by taxi drivers heckling me for their trade. "Cuanta Cueste para Cartagena Vieja?" I tentatively asked. A swarthy, thin-faced man grabbed my bag shouting "Five Dollar, Five Dollar". Sounds OK, I thought and followed him. There is a short drive into town, and remember I have been travelling nearly 30 hours, and although it is now 8pm here, for me it is two in the morning and I haven't seen a bed for over two days, so mistakes can happen. So, we arrive into the old town and he asks my address. "Casa Mamallena I say, Calle Media Luna"

"Que?"

I repeat, several times, thanking my good luck for choosing Manuel from Fawlty Towers.

We drive into the old town, and up and down a variety of streets which are one way, or blocked for road works, or both, finally arriving at the bottom of the road adjacent to the Mamallena location.

"Fifty Dollar!" demands Manuel.

"But you said five dollar, this is a rip off!"

"No rip off. From airport to old town, 50 dollar. You not hear. 50 dollar" he demands, menacingly, but with an insistent smile.

"I'll give you 15 dollar only!" I tried to sound confident, got out of the car, retrieved my bag, gave him three five dollar bills, and made my way around the corner to the Mamallena, pleased that I had got away with my original car rate.

"You should only have given him five dollars. It is the town council agreed rate from the airport. If he charged more he can lose his licence" the kindly old lady at the reception assured me, forgetting it was her hostal who had agreed the $15 rate with me. Oh well, ripped off again, not the first time, and won't be the last.

I dropped off my bag and made my way into the square at the top of the street. There was a shop on the corner selling ice cold beer bottles for just a few pesos, and a party going on. I sat on a bench under a spreading tree and was amazed that in each of the corners of this tiny square there was music playing, people dancing, laughing and generally swinging along to the beat. There were street vendors selling steaming patties, and the most vibrant of atmospheres. A couple more beers and my body clock took over, forcing me to an early bed.

Thankfully, I was up at dawn and ready to walk the sights of the town. Cartagena is built on a grid system, so it is fairly easy to find your way around, and there are delightful shaded little squares everywhere. Separating the town from the beach is a wide city wall, evidently built for protection from British piracy 400 or so years ago. The wall, or ramparts, actually encircles the old town, and I had walked it and some of the squares before taking breakfast at a small bar. The architecture is very colonial and colourful. There is money here because nothing is run down, everywhere spotless and brightly painted and decorated. The frontages of bars, the shops, the offices, the churches, all balustrades and bright statuary. Actually there are statues everywhere from old fashioned stone sculptures to modern iron forged depictions of families, birds, animals, and even one delightfully fat and naked reclining lady who looked very pleased with the world. When she sings it'll be all over, I thought.

My plan, after a first night in Cartagena, was to go to Punta Arena on the Island of Tierra Bomba for snorkelling and relaxation before making my way to Santa Marta for the trek to the lost city.

I collected my bag, and took a taxi to "the beach behind the hospital where the Capitan will be waiting for you" as the kindly old lady had instructed.

The taxi cost $5, but I could have walked it.

On the beach I am greeted by Mateo, the captain of the Cobia 1, a small blue barca (barque), pulled up onto the beach awaiting passengers.

"Wait here 10 minutes, I get gas," said Mateo, and he humped a jerry can on his shoulder and vanished. I stood in the shade of a small tree (the sun is already too fierce, at 9am) and waited for an hour. Fellow shelterers passed the time of day ignoring the gringo except for the occasional shy smile and embarrassed shrug. Mateo eventually returns, ushers me aboard, and we make the short crossing to where I had planned two nights.

My new accommodation is a laid back, shack style hostel with blue and white painted boardwalks linking bunk house to bar to reception to beach. It is a perfect beach bum location so I set to work becoming a beach bum by locating under a palm tree to chill and watch the world go by

I quickly become reacquainted with old friends; diving pelicans, soaring frigate birds, posing egrets and whistling drongos. There is also a large black pig and a family of dogs. Every so often I retreat into the sea to cool off, but it is murky here, with no reef. Snorkelling would have to wait. I would also escape into the sea to avoid the unwanted attention of the masseuses. There were two or three on this beach, but I was to learn they were the same whichever beach you frequented. Large black women with big busts, big bellies and big bottoms dressed in tight top and shorts who would insist on massaging your shoulders even though you have said no thank you any number of times. They are smiling and laughing and talking constantly in some sort of Spanish patois to each other whilst their hands are continually seeking out knots and stiffness in all sorts of private places. Chilling was becoming increasingly difficult.

"No, there is no coral here," confirmed Pedro, the tall, handsome patron of the Beach Hotel, "You must go to Baja Chico on the other side of the island. I'll see if a boy can take you on his motorbike".

So I continued to watch the world go by. From my vantage I could see across the strait to the historic old town, grey stone and low rise, to my left, or south east, then the new Cartagena; an ugly mass of Trump style towers of white condominiums and office blocks, reminding me a little of down town Miami, then to the south west I could see the gibbets and cranes of the docks. There was obviously money here; a lot of investment, and a growing wealth, all built on the back of their newest venture, cultivating over 1,600 varieties of flowers and selling them to more than 90 countries.

As I marvelled at the plunging pelicans a huge container ship hove into view heading, or so I thought for the docks. It was so big I could see its name through my binoculars; the Hamburg Sud. It completely ignored the docks and slowly passed in front of the island, heading East, then turned towards the new town, full circle, then crossed its path heading for the old town, then turned North, passed me on the island and headed back out for the open sea, once again ignoring the dockyard...? What was all that about? This monster ship had entered the strait from nowhere, exercised a perfect figure of eight, and exited the same way it had come in. I was flabbergasted, but it passed the rest of the morning.

Sometime during the afternoon, in between reading, dozing, swimming and fighting off the masseuses, Pedro sought me out, "It is too dangerous to go to the other side of the island on motorbike, so I have arranged that you go by boat with family after breakfast tomorrow. The family want to see the fort at Baja Chico" he explained, "It is much safer than bike," he assured me.

Now, I know everyone enjoys a spell on the beach, and it seemed like a decent idea at the time, but as the afternoon passed slowly and quietly, I was already beginning to regret my decision to leave the lively Hispanic-Caribbean atmosphere of Cartagena, full of bars, restaurants, snack vendors and street theatre, for this, what I could only describe as dead beach with murky seawater and even murkier inhabitants. I even had to leave the beach and wake up the receptionist to get a beer. As twilight approached there was only me and two fishermen left, and they weren't drinking. Worse, as the twinkling lights of the town brightened the gloom in the distance, Pedro appeared to say he had closed the kitchen, but I could have a sandwich before 9 when he went to bed. "I will also have to close the bar!" he added dolefully,

At breakfast next day, Pedro joins me, "I am afraid the daughter of the family is unwell, and they will no longer go to Baja Chico, but do not worry, you will still go."

So straight after downing my third coffee I get my excursion accoutrements together; snorkel, mask, fins, hat, glasses, sunscreen, and made my way down the beach to the blue barca where Mateo sits idly.

"We going to Baja Chico?" I venture enthusiastically, but Mateo shrugs negatively and gestures behind me. I look around and see Pedro stood with his arm around a young black boy, smiling. The boy, who looks no older than 15, is wearing a red t-shirt, jeans and seated solemnly astride a motorcycle

"Hello Ghee-off," Pedro has excellent English, but having seen my name on my passport insists on using the hard Gee, "We cannot send the boat for one person, so Pablo will take you."

I panic momentarily and wonder whether I'm insured for this, then decided to throw caution to the wind. I handed him my things, expecting him to put it in a knapsack or pannier, but he waits till I am sitting on the pillion, and hands them back to me. I found some sort of handhold behind me with my spare hand, and with a slight lurch (from me) off we went.

We began on a narrow track behind the beach, expertly avoiding rocky outcrops, trees, roots, overhanging branches; swerving in and out of shacks and generally avoiding the detritus of driftwood, plastic and broken beach furniture which litter such places. Soon we turn inland and the track gets no wider as we weave through dried mangroves, then we're on a clifftop with precipitous drops onto jagged rocks mere inches to our right. Every so often there's oncoming traffic; other bikes, toddlers walking with mums, donkeys, dogs...Pablo beeps but doesn't slow as we pass on whichever logical side presents itself in that last split second. Its hair raising, exciting and scary all in one, although in truth we probably never go more than 10mph. Occasionally the ascents are so difficult I have to get off and walk, but on the descents we just lean back and stand on the brakes. We go through a couple of desperately poor villages in which there are only black faces to be seen, and I begin to formulate a theory about Colombia's two tier society.

We breast one more climb past green fields strewn with plastic bags, then Baja Chico is down in front of us, a wide sandy bay with, to my fairly trained eye, no sign of a reef of any kind. We ride down onto a desolate beach with the broken down remains of beach huts and dotted with long since closed hotels. No doubt, there was once a vibrant tourist industry here; no more.

I had assumed Pablo to be mute as he had only communicated with me in gestures, and now he gestured out to a solitary white post sticking out about 200 yards off the beach, accommodating a lone pelican. Then his arm swept left to the headland and I assumed this was the area I needed to explore. There were medium sized breakers, but nothing to indicate a tide coming in or out, so I donned my equipment and swam in the direction indicated. Nothing, just sand. I looked up, and Pedro was stood on the rocks indicating I should swim in a larger arc, which I did, but the water just got deeper and murkier; no rocks, no weed, no coral, no fish, nothing.

Back at the bike, Pablo was chatting (yes, chatting), to a local who seemed to suggest we try the other end of the beach. Pablo indicated that I should follow, and he sped off whilst I dripped along behind (I guess he didn't want to get his bike wet). I re-fitted my fins and set off again. It was worse, murkier; I couldn't see more than two feet in front of my mask. Defeated, we headed home, and the journey was no less exhilarating. Pablo, still sullen, received his payment from Pedro and sped off wordlessly. I tell Pedro I'll be checking out and returning to the mainland after lunch.

Back in Cartagena, not so much the land of the living, but more the land of the partying. The Mamollena is full so I find a bed at the Green House Hostal and organise my bus for Santa Marta the next morning. I set off once again to enjoy the delights of this wonderful city and am beginning to understand its orientation. Behind the beach, where I had just landed, is the hospital, and behind that a bridge over an inlet of the sea, then there is the walled town with a variety of gates leading in to the narrow streets. Around each gate there are small markets, because that is where people congregate, and behind each gate there are steps leading up onto the ramparts. All along the ramparts are lovely views out to sea, and in some areas they are nearly 40 yards wide. Here is where the real partying takes place, so here is where I settle down for the evening's entertainment.

Down in the plazas is where people eat and congregate for light socialising, so that is where you will find the violinist, guitarist, string quartet type buskers, playing classical music whilst people sup, a sort of lively yet slightly subdued atmosphere. Here up on the ramparts is where the folk come who can't afford to eat at the swanky restaurants, so there are vendors selling iced drinks, hot dogs, cheese pies, cocktails and honeyed nuts. The raucous bands are up here, the dancers and acrobats and drummers are up here. Everyone's drinking, dancing, laughing; over here is a man with a snake, and over there one with a pet sloth, another has a jaguarina on a lead, and another some pet parrots. You can join in, it's hard not to join in, or just grab a beer for a few pesos and go and sit on a cannon and look out to a sea streaked with moonbeams or up to the star splashed sky, and in the warm, balmy, fun-filled atmosphere wonder at why you would ever want to be anywhere else.

But, somewhere else is where I had to be, so it was the next morning I am seated in the Green House reception awaiting an eight o'clock bus to Santa Marta. Outside a gang of workmen are fixing street lights and they have blocked off the road. So I am worried my shuttle can't get to me. The receptionist can't help, she has no English and is a different girl to the one who'd made the reservation for me last evening.

"El autobus de Marisol para Santa Marta, ven aqui?" I would ask; is it coming here? She would just smile and shrug. "Es possible telefono?" She shook her head and pointed outside. The upshot was that the shuttle couldn't come to pick me up because the road was closed, we couldn't telephone to rearrange because the phones were down, and we couldn't email either as there was no wifi because the electricity is off. All because they were working on the street lights outside.

"Why are they doing repairs anyway, it's Sunday morning at 8 o'clock, for goodness sake!!!" I felt like shouting. But I didn't, I just fretted I wasn't going to get to Santa Marta. Then this wizened old guy trolls in. He's wearing cut off jeans, a frayed straw hat, an official navy blue t-shirt and a name plate hung around his neck proclaiming him to be Nick. "You for the Rosario Islands?" he asks in a Spanish American accent. The couple, who I hadn't noticed, but were on the next sofa leapt up and grab their bags.

"No, I am trying to go to Santa Marta, but Marisol keep not arriving, and I have to be there by six," I sort of protested.

"OK. Don't worry. You wait here. I will take you in 20 minutes," he sounded reassuring, but this is how scams and rip-offs start.

"But what if Marisol turns up," I protested pleadingly.

He turned to me like a kindly old teacher, "Look, I have spent the last 30 years of my life ripping off Americans. Trust me, I'll get you onto the Santa Marta bus."

The upshot was, Nick took me in a taxi to Berlinas Coach station for $6, bought me the ticket for $36, $10 dollars cheaper than Marisol, and charged me $6 dollars for his time. So I'd been ripped off to the tune of $2. Robbing basket.

Santa Marta

It was a wonderful four-hour journey along the shores of the Caribbean. We stopped briefly in a city called Barranquilla and when I got back on the bus the conductress rather got my name stuck in her throat as she tried a roll call. I'm not surprised, she'd got me down as Gesttrez Leo. After Barranquilla we travelled over a series of bridges and islands to pass a major inlet of the Caribbean called the Cienaga Grande de Santa Marta, then the beach resort of Rodadero before climbing a headland with suddenly Santa Marta appearing sprawling below us. The passengers told the driver to drop me off at my destination, the Hotel Teyronne, where waiting in reception was Mark, our guide.

He had already met up with Jolien a delightfully intelligent, pretty 20 something Dutch girl whose English was not only far better than mine, she could also hilariously affect a perfect 'Essex Girl' accent, which she used "...to discourage any unwanted attention. It works every time." Mark was an affable, well-built Englishman, had studied at The University of Birmingham and supported Aston Villa, but lived in Bogotá with his wife and young son.
"You like football, Geoff?"
I said I did, so he whisked the two of us off to a seafront restaurant for a huge lunch of rice and various meats, a Bandeja Paisa, swilled down with beer, as we watched

Colombia being beaten 1-0 by their neighbours and fiercest rivals, Venezuela in the Copa America. You'd have thought the result would have quietened down the locals. But they were as happy, jovial and friendly as ever. They weren't going to allow a mere football match spoil their national pastime and philosophy; party!

After an afternoon spent sleeping off the lunch, I had been instructed to present myself at the rooftop bar of the hotel at six, when we would meet up with the other members of our expedition.

So, there's Mark, Jo, and myself. Then Jonathan; a tall, strong young man who laboured under an unforgiving stammer. He was from Liverpool and explained (eventually) how his stutter was always worse when he first met people. We worked tirelessly to help him overcome his problem, but it was difficult and we realised how easy it was to fall into a group conversation where Jonathan was just completely left out. Thank goodness for social media which allows him to converse effortlessly.

Perran, English, professional backpacker; Amy, Canadian dental hygienist, and Brooke, American cabin crew, are all in their twenties, while Denise is a Canadian professor having five days off from a medical convention in Mexico, and is the only one within 10 years of my age. Tara is a character. She is also Canadian, 30 something, and one of those northerners who really enjoy their ten month winters. She is blonde, but has dyed her hair black to avoid harassment, and her first comment having introduced herself as "Terra", (or even "Terror" as in George Bush's war on Terrorism, pronounced tourism!) was "I love the way you British pronounce my name with the long 'a'" She further enhanced her eccentricities to us when at dinner she ordered risotto "but with no rice".

Mark briefed us on our equipment requirements for the following day, explained that our Indian guide, Celsio, would be joining us, then whisked us away for dinner in quite a posh restaurant. I had a rather delicious sea bass in orange sauce, I haven't a clue what Tara ended up with, but for the next week it was going to be rice and beans for all of us.

There was a special moment at the end of the meal which had the group roaring with laughter to Tara's bemusement. She had ordered a cake which came decorated with a glace cherry. Totally innocently she asked "Would anyone like my cherry?" (titters) "Geoff, will you take my cherry?" ("No, thanks!" I spluttered trying to suppress muffled giggles) "Jonathan, surely you'd like to have my cherry?" The table fell about. Children!

La Ciudad Perdida

The next day began with a two-hour bus journey along the coast and past the the Parque Tayrona, a protected area for the tribes, then we transferred into a 4 x 4 for a bouncy journey up into the foothills of the Sierra Nevada. Stopping at the village of Machete Pelau we took lunch and were introduced to our guide, Celsio who, aided by Mark gave us an introduction into the indigenous people.

There are four tribes of the Teyrunna or Santa Marta Mountain Indians; the Wiwa , Kogi, Aranhuaco and Manuaco. Their's is a Mother Earth philosophy, they look after their own health and education, jealously guard their culture and settlements, and only allow archaeologists and expeditions to their lost city as it follows an ancient mule trail. All wear white, never cut their hair, women and girls work in the home and fields, men and boys 'provide' for the family and play. The coca leaf is a very important part of their culture in both fertility, leisure and bonding with Mother Earth. For this the government allow them to cultivate the coca tree.

Celsio was an elder of the Wiwa tribe. To complement his white three quarter trousers and loose jacket, woven from local fibres, he wore a wide brimmed white sombrero. When he removed this to go swimming he revealed glossy black hair that reached down to his backside. He was quietly spoken with a calm demeanour, and unusual for his tribe, bilingual, and Mark could translate for us from his Spanish. In a pouch called a poporo he carried coca leaves mixed with seashells which he constantly ground with a ceremonial stick, occasionally wiping the contents around his gums to augment the ever present wad of chewed coca leaves. I fell in love with him immediately he explained to us that in his language humming birds are called flower kissers.

The trek began quite easily and sedately as we walked along the Buritaca river. It was a winding but easy trail down the valley, using the shade of the canopy to keep the burning sun off us. Sometimes we had to clamber up and over rocks, but the atmosphere was relaxed and the conversations good. We even stopped after an hour for a swim. We were assuredly lulled into a false state of tranquillity.

Then we crossed the river and began to climb. The canopy disappeared and the sun baked us. The ancient trail cuts deep into the hillside, at times forming gullies ten feet deep. But the climb was relentless, up and up and up, out of the river valley. Thankfully we lost the sun, but the heat and humidity took their toll. The group had strung out, but Mark had stayed with me, assuring that this was the hardest part. It was plod and rest, legs beginning to feel like jelly, I am feeling my age, as we zig-zag ever upwards.

Eventually we breasted the crest, and there is a kiosk from which I purchased an ice cold Gatorade. For the next hour we walked along this ridge with wonderful views of the forested high sierra on both sides. I buddied up with Tara and we swapped stories of family life in our respective countries. Every so often the local Indians provide a table of fresh fruit for which they are paid by the guides from a previously amassed kitty. It was after a particularly welcome table of refreshing watermelon next to a blue school building that we began the descent into camp Adan for our first night. I couldn't believe we had endured that great climb out of the Buritaca valley to then descend back into it. The ancient mule drivers must have known what they were doing.

I reached the river again, crossed a rickety old bridge and collapsed onto a bunk, exhausted. It was six o'clock. But before dinner Mark had promised another swimming opportunity. Costumes on, back over the rickety bridge and 20 minutes over and around boulders to the pool. A heart stopping 20-foot leap into the river, splash around, marvel at the fish which had mini feeding frenzies every time you spat into the pool, then haul yourself out for another exciting leap. This didn't last long. Bodies were craving for food and sleep. Chicken dinner, one beer, then haul yourself under the mosquito net, and gone.

Up at 4:30, breakfast at 5:30, pack up then off for what Mark assures us is a short but hard ascent. Three hours later after an irresistible climb back out of the valley, and I am exhausted. I have evidently still not recovered from the previous day. Denise has loaned me one of her sticks. "If you're right handed, I'll take your left stick, if that's alright" I said, cheekily. Denise looked confused. Canadians, much like their American cousins, have difficulty with humour, especially irony and sarcasm. But this pathetic attempt on my part fell on totally stony ground as she, quite seriously looked at her sticks, then her hands in puzzlement, then offered me both saying "You can have whichever is easier." I chose one and thanked her graciously. It's unfair to mock someone who is genuinely trying to help an obviously distressed old man.

So, once again it has been a long painful ascent, until we crest a ridge, where watermelon awaits, then thankfully we began

the long but much easier route down into a Wiwa village.
Tonight we sleep in hammocks.

The beauty of a shallow, downhill slope is that you are not
having to concentrate on struggling to put one foot in front of
the other. You can look around at the magnificent views, stop
to admire and smell the flowers, enjoy the birds and
butterflies, feel the peace and solitude of being at one with
nature. The downside of a downhill slope is that you know for
every stride down there's going to be at least two strength
sapping steps up; also the knowledge that in a few days' time,
this languid downhill stroll will become a long uphill slog.

We arrive into the village in time for a light, late lunch after
which we go down to the river. After a few minutes splashing
about, and easing the aching limbs in the cool waters,
everyone else begins to explore up and down stream, I find a
flat rock to crawl out onto and snooze in the sunshine.

Later that afternoon Celsio takes us into the village fields to
show us how they cultivate coffee, cacao, banana, maize and
coca. Butterflies and humming birds are fluttering and
humming all around us and the scene seems so idyllic in this
Shangri La valley surrounded by almost impenetrable forested
slopes, but these villagers seem so poor, at least in our
definition of the word. To them, and indeed to many more
they have riches aplenty.

Back at camp some boys are playing football and we join in.
After a fish dinner Mark has organised a night safari into the
jungle. We kit up; boots, long trousers and sleeves, plenty of
repellent, and head torches. Mark walks us down to the river
pointing out the eye-shine of creatures on the way; mainly
spiders and frogs, perhaps the occasional rat or snake. We
walk along the river for some time, then turn left into the
undergrowth and follow a tiny tributary upstream. This is
dense jungle, full of treacherous creepers, roots and rocks. I'm
at the back of the group so that anything that is spotted is long

gone by the time I get there. This dejected feeling affects my concentration and a rock wobbles under my foot. I try to steady myself by putting my other foot on a more solid rock, but it is slimy and I can't get a foothold. With both feet decidedly unsteady, my body begins to sway and I look for a branch, or (selfishly) another person to grasp onto. With neither forthcoming and arms flailing absurdly I fall backwards and sit heavily down into the stream, soaked up to my waist. Now I am really pissed off.

Again, back at camp, but this time I am desperately trying to dry my boots, my last pair of socks, and my trousers (not so critical). Around the long table some of the others are trying to get a game of cards going and Jo tells us of an encounter she had in the washroom of the Plaza hotel in New York. She was just washing her hands as someone left the bathroom (?). The woman at the next sink suddenly grabbed Jo's arm and said "That was Amy Robach, did you see her? That was Amy Robach!"

"Who?" said Jo, trying to extricate her arm from the excited grasp.

"Amy Robach, (pause) AMY ROBACH, from Good Morning America," came the almost breathless reply.

"I'm sorry, I don't know who Amy Robach is," Jo tried to explain calmly.

"Amy Robach....from Good Morning America....you must know her...(and her voice rose again)...*Amy Robach*...from *Good Morning America.*" Jo faced her with an expressionless look, and then the penny seemed to drop for the excitable American woman; "Don't you watch Good Morning America?" she asked, incredulously.

"No, I'm from the Netherlands, in Europe," explained Jo.

"Well, don't you have Good Morning America there?" she continued, disbelievingly.

"Er, No, for two very good reasons," Jo explained soberly. "First, we are the Netherlands, not America, and secondly when it is on here for you, for us it is already the afternoon!" and with that Jo turned and left the washroom, leaving the woman standing there, mouth open in astonishment.

Americans, they are always a fund of anecdotes. Even Tara laughed with a mixture of delight and embarrassment at her American cousins. "Canadians", she said, "We are like America Light!"

As a group we turned into our hammocks. Soon I could hear gentle snoring all around, but I couldn't sleep worrying that my boots and socks would still be too wet in the morning and would hamper the trek. I'd done this before, when climbing Kilimanjaro some years before; I had lain awake worrying over whether I had packed enough underwear! The really mundane plagues at your senses when you are at altitude.

Seemingly moments later I was being gently rocked awake from my cocoon. It was Celsio, passing amongst the hammocks, just touching the securing ropes enough to rock us out of our slumber, and humming gently to himself.

The first thing I did was to find my socks above the dying embers of the fire. They were still wet, I fretted, until Mark told me to snap out of it "Your feet will be soaked with sweat in five minutes anyway. Stop being a wus and just get your boots on."

I couldn't believe I had made such a fuss. Socks, underwear; we're on a climbing expedition. Nobody cares what you look like or smell like. Just get the job done!

We left the village to begin day three of the trek shortly after a breakfast of eggs, porridge and toast. The sun was barely up and the cool of the day appreciated. It took us only an hour along the river bank before we reached a perfect swimming pool and launched into it. Above us was a green iron bridge. Across this and we began to climb again, inexorably following this damn mule trail. This was a four-hour brutal climb. We are climbing a ridge, with great views of mile after mile of jungle on both sides, but it is difficult to appreciate it as you struggle to put one foot just slightly in front of the other. Thankfully we are under canopy so out of the merciless sun. However, the canopy keeps off any breeze, and the heat and humidity are cruel. You cannot keep anything dry as you sweat profusely. It is also lonely, we are strung out, perhaps no more than ten yards apart, but it may as well be hundreds as it is impossible to strike up any conversation and your eyes can only be focussed on the next step.

Finally, at the top and we feast on biscuits, pineapple and sugar cane. There is an army presence reminding us of the potentially volatile nature of these remote mountains; a few young lads in loose uniform and rifles, lazing in the shade of the sparse trees growing at the peak of the trail.

Then the down starts, but I am not ready, my legs still like jelly, my lungs complaining, I am tired and in need of more rest. We are descending for the last time back into the river valley. There is quite a lot of scrambling and hauling of tired bodies over boulders with landings which truly jar the knees. I have fallen behind and sometimes cannot see the best route to follow. I begin to feel very alone, aware that eyes could be watching which have menacing motives. All predators will follow a herd and try to pick off the weak and defenceless, and currently I am the old, infirm wildebeest cut off from the herd which wild dogs will work at harassing until down and then dead. There are no wild dogs, or wolves, or lion, or tiger, or leopard here, but there are jaguar, and it would indeed be their lucky day if they could catch up and stalk my apparent frailty. The paranoia is working perfectly when I spot vultures circling above.

I eventually catch up with the group at a river crossing. This would normally be forded, but rains somewhere up stream have turned it into a raging torrent and we have to use a precarious pulley and chair contraption built to carry one person at a time. I am able to help with the 'pulleying' of people across the river, after all what little strength I have left is in my arms, and I am the (last to arrive, therefore) last to cross. The chair is really a rusted, overlarge canary cage which swings crazily as the pulley works its magic. There is now just 45 minutes to camp, but half way there and Mark has to hang back and help me across some of the more difficult terrain. At one stage we had just hauled ourselves up over an enormous boulder when behind us there is a sudden crack like a clap of thunder. We turn to see a huge bough we had passed under seconds ago, snap and clatter heavily onto the rocks; a lucky escape.

In Paradise Camp I find a cot and crawl under the mosquito net to rest my aching limbs. Sometime in the evening I emerged briefly for rice and beans, but I intended to sleep for most of the 12 hours we had before our dawn ascent up the famous 1200 steps into the lost city itself.

Our assault on Teyruna began with a precarious hike up river in absolute darkness. This is no towpath, we have to clamber over and around huge boulders deposited when the river was much bigger over millions of years. Dawn was beginning to break as we forded the river for the last leg of our expedition. There was not much more light though as we were shrouded in deep canopy. We found the first of the slithery stone steps and began the climb. This entrance to the hitherto unknown city was found by illegal bird looters in 1972. The opportunistic bird thieves proceeded to strip the city of its riches before announcing their find to the world of archaeology. We'll never know what treasures they stole but the descendants of the Tairuna people believe in the karma of

Mother Earth and they watched from a distance as the thieves fell out. The only survivor was apparently a wizened old adventurer by the name of Fernando Rey who escaped to Cuba after shooting dead his partner.

The climb was never going to be easy. Pole Pole ...Pole Pole, the Swahili description of slowly putting one foot in front of the other; a Polar Plod as Ranulph Fiennes would describe it. We're not in Africa, nor Antarctica, but the same philosophy applies. You can't rush, or make big strides; four or five small steps, and rest. At one stage I looked up and there are four figures dressed all in white with long flowing black hair. Angels come for me? No, Wiwa children on their way to school..

We arrive at a clearing and the land is terraced with the foundations of a circular building. Celsio explains this is the entrance and leads us in a walking ceremony, closing the circle, a ritual to assure Mother Earth of our peaceful intentions, positioning her omnipresence in the centre of our being.

Then there are more steps as the jungle begins to clear, there are more foundations, and it is clear we are in the middle of what was once a large community. We climb to the very top, turn and take in the most wonderful panorama. The city laid out in terraces below us and all around the green, forested mountains. There is a small army presence here also, and some of the boys (soldiers) were only too happy to pose for photographs.

Celsio was now in his element. He led us on secret pathways, showed us a holy waterfall, introduced us to a local shaman, a mama, who blessed us and showed us a boulder with map like lines etched on its surface. What we might call ley lines, proved, according to Celsio that this particular lost city was linked in some way to another famous lost city on the same continent, Machu Pichu. Sounds fantasy to me. Built by different peoples (the Inca), and separated not only by most of the continent, but also by over 600 years (this one was older), the one thing the places had in common, other than being lost, was that they were both abandoned because of the Spanish Conquest, in Machu Pichu's case to protect its discovery, and for Teyuna because of diseases the white Europeans had brought with them.

It is impossible not to compare the two cities, and both of the arduous treks needed to reach them. M P has a more ethereal feel, is more complete, and the trek through the Andes is more spectacular. Trekking the Inca Trail via the Sacred Valley takes you into the cloud forest. Here it is all rainforest. But they are two different civilisations; the Inca had an empire but are now extinct, whereas the Tairuna are very much alive and thriving, thanks, in no small measure to the four tribes of the Santa Marta mountains, and their ability to live alongside the New World, albeit displaying an air of superiority.

We breakfasted on arepas we had brought with us, then suitably refreshed began the return. In my mind's eye I could now envisage our task. The route will take us down to the river, then follow the river to Paradise camp, then further along until we cross the river at the chair pulley. We then have a long climb up past the banana plantations to the small army camp, where we will take on fruit refreshments, then the really long descent down to the green bridge. It was on this descent I came across climbers coming the other way and felt dreadfully sorry for them and their gasping sweating endeavour. Their red agonised expressions, lifting their heads painfully to receive a crumb of comfort from the happy downhill plodder, "Nearly half way" I would lie, grinning reassuringly.

The other side of the green bridge there was a swimming opportunity, taken gratefully. Celsio showed us the undersides of rocks where six inch spiders awaited sun down, the time to hunt. We dried and dressed and took the long, easy, undulating trek in the cool of the late afternoon back to the Wiwa village. This final part of a long day on the trail was my favourite. There was plenty of shade, we knew that enveloping hammocks hung gently swaying ready to welcome us, and the birds sang while butterflies danced our route along the riverside.

The difference was; we had previously had to work to achieve an unknown goal. Having accomplish this goal, with success and our victory behind us, we could afford the luxury of a little spring to our step knowing there were no more ascents, at least not today.

We pass some roundel homesteads, straw villages with children playing happily in the dirt. A giant, electric blue butterfly seems intent on landing on me, and as dusk approaches fire flies make shooting stars through the trees and flowering shrubs.

Dinner that night had added ingredients to the rice and beans; pasta with strips of meat; "Gato!" insisted our cook, Alphonso, with a smile. Cat!

I played the Oreo game (fingers on the biscuit, twist, whoever gets the cream, wins)with Tara and Jo and lost as usual. However the atmosphere in camp is a little subdued as Mark and Perran have taken to their beds feeling ill, both putting it down to the sun. "A little sunstroke", people say euphemistically. It's no joke!

The final day has an up, a down to camp Adan, a big up, and then down to the river and along to Machete Pelao where we will pick up our vehicles to take us back to civilisation and a hotel bed in Santa Marta.

We begin at dawn after a breakfast of arepas. It is a long, upward, tortuous, zig-zag plod. It may be the coolest part of the day but you are soaked in sweat after only ten minutes.

The views are wonderful as the sun slowly uncovers the mountain tops and wisps of cloud still inhabit the valleys. At night you have the chirrup of the frogs, but in the day the cicadas take over, and as the day warms up their shrill gets louder as tiny colourful butterflies seem to urge you on, fluttering in front of your painful ascent.

We paused for a moment at the top, to take on water and drink in the views, then haul on the backpack (which I'm convinced is getting heavier, but not many more hauls left), and set off down the track. It is an hour before we reach Adan, load up with fruit, biscuits and juice, but don't linger, as we cross over the rickety old bridge and face the last ascent.

It is a relief to reach to the blue school building and there is a long walk along the ridge before the final descent. To my right are families of howler monkeys, below me but up in the canopy. I am accompanied on this walk by their constant growling and grunting. I have happily fallen behind, pausing to look for the monkeys in the canopy with my binoculars, but having no luck. I'm in no rush now. This has been one of the most difficult treks I have ever undertaken, with its constant ascents and descents, up and out of, then back down into river valleys, on difficult terrain through humid and hot jungle interspersed with baking sun on winding paths. Now I'm taking it easy. Even Mark and Perran both still feeling under the weather are ahead of me. Then I catch up with Jonathan, and he is struggling.
The big lad has discarded his boots, he can no longer fit his swollen blistered feet inside them, and he is struggling over the stony ground in his stockinged feet, wincing with every step.

"Here!" I say, and swing my backpack to the ground, "Use these" and I untied my flip flops (without the toe piece, which I find so uncomfortable) and offered them to him.
"Aah! Bliss!" he eventually managed to say after trying them for a few steps, and I knew I'd made a friend for life.

We finished the journey together, and found the rest of the group waiting for us at the cafe where it all began. The first thing I do is find a standing tap and plunge my overheated head under its cold gushings, then for that "Ice Cold in Alex" moment; The Beer.

Three hours later after repeating the 4WD and minibus drive back we're in the hotel and I am showering and gently removing ticks from my weary body. We dine that night at a posh fish restaurant where I had fillet steaks in blue cheese then Mark takes us to a rooftop bar where quite frankly it is too windy. I just want my bed.

Overnight several more ticks simply bloat and drop off, we lose Brooke, Denise and Amy to early flights, and decide over breakfast to go to the beach.

Beach Life Colombian Style is something to be experienced!

We had taken a taxi to Rodadero beach, around the western headland of Santa Marta. Even early morning the sun has baked the sand so it is too hot to walk on barefoot The sea is tropical warm, that is to say never below 27 degrees, and music is playing, that is dance, beat, samba music. Tents line the beach, each one with six beach beds. We settle down and within seconds our own personal beer vendor introduces himself to us, and he'll be here every half an hour to sell us an ice cold Aguila for 75p. Then the massage girls appear, all as I have previously described, black with tight shorts and shirt hardly covering huge bellies, bottoms and boobs, hair tied back in colourful scarves, and they chat and laugh excitedly in patois amongst themselves as they invade you naughtily with their hands.

Luckily, Mark's Spanish is good enough to admonish them with a few harsh words, but they simply identify him as the leader and three descend on him to concentrate on his weak spots. Then Manolito our beer boy turns up again.

The beach is buzzing, music playing, Bob Marley at least every other track. Brightly coloured cocktail boats are wheeled about, machetes being wielded with abandon to open coconuts for Coca-Locas or Pina Coladas; and they're selling food; arepas, ice creams, fruit, snacks, nuts, rice cakes. You never need to leave your tent except to cool off in the Caribbean or play on the bananas, donuts or jet skis.

Having said all that, there is no such thing as relaxing on the beach. This is Colombia; it is party, party, party.

Sadly, late afternoon, I must leave Mark, Perran, Jonathan, Jo and Tara to the beach life as I board a bus back to Cartagena. A day wandering the wonderful streets of this Caribbean gem then flights to Bogota, Madrid and finally home.

One last little mishap though. I had a seven-hour layover in Bogota so decided to avail myself of the first class lounge. $30 dollars to eat as much as you like, imbibe fine wines and laze about in absolute top notch comfort. I fell asleep, and woke at 17:02. My flight was 17:20. Absolute panic as I grabbed all my gear and high tailed it for the boarding gate. I made it, but in absolute agony having stubbed my toes on the floor flap you raise to plug in your mobile phone.

Three days earlier I had slept in a village in the jungle, amongst the mountains of an ancient land and had been gently raised from my slumber by an indigenous Indian as he softly sang and rocked my hammock.

*

Peru and Peru Again

In my childhood we were brought up on Westerns. On TV, at the cinema, and in books, it was all Cowboys and Indians. It was only with James Fennymore Cooper's *Last of the Mohicans* that we learnt there was a different type of America, one with British and French influence, and we discovered Iriqois and Inuit and the Pathfinder Hawkeye (similar raccoon hat to Davy Crocket, I believe).

History, as it was portrayed, had the White Man and the Indians; goodies and baddies, and it was as simple as that. There was some sympathy for the "Red Indian", but only if they stayed on their reservations and collaborated. We discovered tribes such as Cheyenne, Cherokee, Apache, Navajo, and many more. Names like Buffalo Bill, Geronimo, Colonel Custer, Crazy Horse and Sitting Bull became childhood heroes. I even remember a board game based upon the Battle of the Little Big Horn.

There were fictitious heroes as well; Hopalong Cassidy and Roy Rogers were two favourites. We got to know their theme tunes and even their horses. The Lone Ranger had the William Tell Overture and Silver. He also had a sidekick, a Comanche Indian named Tonto. As proof of our attitudes to what we now call Native Americans, Tonto means stupid in Spanish.

But it was always from the viewpoint of the North American tribes, with their wigwams, totem poles, tomahawks and penchant for riding around wagon trains. Mexico featured in the Alamo, and as a place for outlaws to escape, but that was it. And as far as black people were concerned, they were slaves on plantations like Tara (Gone with the Wind), and hardly featured in the taming of the west, until Blazing Saddles. Now we know it was so different.

Later names such as Aztecs, Olmecs, Maya and the Inca became part of my childhood. New names appeared like Cortes, Pizarro and Montezuma, and we learned of civilizations and great cities, religious worship and human sacrifice. We never associated these people with the generally nomadic tribes of the north, and indeed when we read in National Geographic about lost tribes in the Amazon Rainforest, naked and using blowpipes, these were also seen as a completely separate race of people.

Enlightened times have shown us that all of the people of the Americas are descended from those who crossed the land bridge of the Bering Strait across the millennia, after we had come out of Africa.

Thor Heyerdahl even showed us in the 1950's how the people of the Andes built reed boats and colonised the islands of the South Pacific. The balsa rafts he built to prove his theory were called Kon Tiki, and were made to designs created by the tribes of Lake Titicaca, the highest navigable lake in the world. Then I heard of a boat, a steamship, commissioned in Birmingham, built in London, transported to this mysterious lake in boxes, and which, whilst I was still at school, steamed up and down between Peru and Bolivia nearly a hundred years later.

I was hooked. I had to visit Lake Titicaca, I had to see this boat, and I needed to learn more about these people of the Americas.

Over my lifetime I have become aware of many heroes of the Americas, names too numerous to mention here, but just a few that followed Davy Crocket and John Wayne were Atticus Finch, Simon Bolivar, Eva Peron, Isabel Allende, Pele, Usain Bolt and Barack Obama. In my twenties I entertained the mad theories of Erich Von Daniken, that "God was an Astronaut" and that the mysterious Lines of Nazca were created for an alien airfield. I have had an interest in these lines and images ever since, which created yet another bucket list item.

And then came Macchu Picchu. Rediscovered by Hiram Bingham in 1911, this lost mountain top Inca city, virtually unknown to the outside world until the late 20th century, has become the most popular tourist attraction of Peru, if not for the whole of South America.

An expedition to trek the Inca Trail to Macchu Picchu became my first incursion into the continent, and for this visit to South America I was still in employment, and could therefore only take time constrained adventures. So even though I would be within touching distance of Lake Titicaca and the Nazca desert, I was only able to include Macchu Picchu. In truth I shouldn't have done that, as most experts say you need at least a week's acclimatisation at altitude before attempting the infamous Inca Trail. I didn't have that luxury, I had nine days, start to finish, and luckily I found an expedition that would take me.

Hence I found myself in the Spring of 2003 (sorry, it's Autumn in the southern hemisphere), seated in a cramped hotel lobby in Lima clutching my bags. It is pre-dawn, and I have the company of about ten fellow adventurers and we are all huddled in the gloom, awaiting the minibus which will take us to the airport for the domestic flight up to Cusco. There are a variety of journeys behind us that have brought us together to this lobby; mine has been three flights overnight, a whistle stop tour of Peru's capital and a fitful few hours kip in this two star hotel. My body clock says it's midday, but I've had about six hours sleep in 36 and it's dark outside.

The last thing I want to be at this juncture is sociable.

Suddenly, a woman steps down into the lobby, she's not unlike Richie Cunningham's mother from Happy Days, all blonde and flouncy, and she has a huge American grin. She approaches the first huddled traveller, thrusts out her hand and declares loudly "Hi, I'm Jane!". The poor young man reluctantly shakes her hand and mumbles. Undeterred, Jane moves onto the next huddled unfortunate and declares again, "Hi, I'm Jane!", shakes the limply proffered hand, and moves on to each of us in turn, "Hi, I'm Jane!" loudly to each, as if the previous declarations had been personal whispers. Eventually, the whole group having been accosted she looks for somewhere to sit, and flounces herself down with an air of breathless satisfaction. Only then am I aware of the small, grey man shuffling apologetically behind her. "Hello, folks, I'm Sam," he says softly, and sits beside her. I smiled briefly at him and almost imperceptibly raised my eyebrows in empathy. Sam caught the body language, nodded and sent a brief smile back with lowered eyes.

The flight to Cusco was only two hours, and the sprawl that greeted us typically South American. A central square with cathedral and two-storied cloisters, gardens with fountains and ubiquitous pigeons, and suburbs climbing the hillsides all around. That evening over a dinner that included Alpaca and Cuy (guinea pig) the group began to gel. There were four Americans, four Aussies, two kiwis and a Canadian. There was another Brit with me and our Peruvian guide Hualca. It was interesting to observe the group dynamics. Generally, the Commonwealth citizens grouped together although the Americans couldn't see that. The Antipodeans became quite close but the Aussies appeared to affect an air of dominance.

The Canadian, feeling sorry for his neighbours, allied himself to the Americans, who weren't aware of the coalition, and we Brits...well we just enjoyed observing the various alliances, as no-one really wanted to ally with us. Colonialism, it appears, is perpetual.

Cusco is at an altitude of 3,400 metres, which is well over 11,000 feet, or more than three times higher than Ben Nevis, Britain's highest mountain. It used to nestle, now it's narrow streets are an exhaust fume choking sprawl. At this height, altitude sickness can be a real problem. Generally, I didn't feel any difference with the thin air, even with the fumes, and just found myself breathing a little heavier after a flight of stairs. However, checking into my hotel room the first thing that happened was a massive nose bleed. This was caused more by the dry air than the altitude, but was still a concern. The thin air also affects sleep. It was already a problem being six hours behind GMT, but when you try to sleep at this altitude, your breathing is at your expected natural low rate. However, with each breath taking in less oxygen, you occasionally find yourself abruptly woken as your lungs demand a sudden extra lungful; a sharp intake of breath.

Day two in the Inca highlands saw the group clambering over the preserved remains of Sacsayhuaman, the old fortified city in the eucalyptus forests above Cusco, and then transported down into the Sacred Valley. This is the fertile valley of the rushing Urubamba river. It is sacred because it exhibits the five holies of the Incas: sun, earth, water, mountains and sky; and mirrors on earth the direction of the Milky Way in the night sky at the summer solstice. There was a stop at the colourful market town of Pisac to lunch and collect supplies, then at the ruins of Ollantaytambo, a natural amphitheatre for more clambering.

We checked into a simple dormitory and fed well before being serenaded with El Condor Pasa. It appears to be written in stone that every musician must play it at least once every hour. I wasn't sick of it yet, but we may soon become so.

The next morning, in glorious sunshine we are taken to kilometre 82 and cross the bridge over the Urubamba to begin our trek on the Inca Trail which would culminate in Macchu Picchu. The first four hours are delightful as we follow flood plain meadows full of butterflies, wild flowers, llamas and humming birds. We picnic next to the river and enjoy a sunny doze before Hualca readies us for our climb.

"We are climbing Dead Woman's pass. See the two mounds pointing skyward at the summit," Hualca himself points skyward through the trees to what appears as a double mountain peak. "Most groups stop halfway, but _we_ will make it to meadows below the summit!" As the iridescent wings of a tiny humming bird glinted in the sunshine behind him, so did his smile radiate into an almost evil grin. "It will be hard work, but *we* will make it. I have good climbers here!" Once again he emphasised the 'we'. We all looked at one another trying to guess to whom he was referring, as the collective penny dropped.

The Inca trail is arduous; not because it is steep, nor due to any challenging terrain or the need to scramble, or scale precipitous heights; no, it is difficult because it is stepped. The trail is fairly narrow, not meant for say, carts, as the Inca never invented or used the wheel. (I've never been a great believer in the wheel as an invention. Sliced bread was much better. Look at unicyclists, and the problems they have getting anywhere. No, the wheel was never a great invention. The axle, however revolutionised transport. The idea of putting two wheels either side of a piece of wood, harnessing a horse, and putting a seat on top and a flatbed behind; that was the innovation that the Inca failed to invent) It is narrow in order for two people to walk side by side, or with a pack animal, say a llama, as the Inca also didn't have the use of the horse or mule. Every five or ten yards of gentle slope, there will be a step of perhaps 18 inches or two feet to haul yourself up. This means you cannot develop a rhythm to the trek; five or six steps then, "Hup!", and at altitude it takes it out of you. Rather than going up a step, the body would much prefer to use it to sit down.

So we began the climb.

It was not long before the party was strung out. Frank, the Canadian with the huge handlebar moustache, was the eldest, giving me at least ten years, and also the heaviest, and he struggled at the back from the start. My fellow Brit, Debbie, was also carrying a little too much and she also found it hard going. I felt for them both, and as is my custom, I brought up the rear to try to encourage them along. Before long Hualca noticed this and dropped back to help Debbie and Frank. He encouraged me to quicken my pace and join the front runners. I did this, but as soon as I caught them where they rested in a wooded glade, they started off again whereas I needed my rest.

And the pattern of the climb continued. Everyone had to find their own pace, it was just too hard to hang yourself back, or try to get ahead. The hike up to Dead Woman's Pass was one you had to battle yourself. Sometimes, especially with the altitude effect, you could only manage a dozen or so small steps, and you had to rest, gasping for the extra oxygen.

As difficult as the walking sometimes was, our surroundings were beautiful. We were climbing up through the cloud forest so everywhere was green. The trees and shrubs were in both leaf and flower; trunks and branches covered with moss or bromeliads, the air was humid but mercifully cool. The sun dappled, and we were always next to or within earshot of a babbling stream or waterfall. Occasionally you could get your head up and look down and across the valley we were climbing out of. It was never less than spectacular, especially with the glacier clad Andes beyond.

The humidity on the lower slopes, and our efforts meant we were saturated with sweat, which cooled when we stopped, making shirts both sticky and cold; very uncomfortable to haul your packs back onto. Every time we stopped we needed to towel down, gulp in oxygen, rest our knees, calves and thighs, and take on water. I had a bamboo walking pole and I couldn't imagine life without it. We fell in love. Years later I still dream of my walking stick and the time we had together.

Progress was slow, but after what seemed an eternity the path widened and I broached a final steep step and found myself in a freezing, boggy meadow. Above I could still see the twin peaks to which we aimed, but I could also see about a mile ahead our tented camp and realised the ordeal of the hike up Dead Woman's Pass was nearly at an end.

I dragged myself that last mile and fell into a tent, any tent, and slept.

A while later I woke from my doze and could hear activity. I roused myself and looked outside. Frank was arriving. I have no idea how long it had been since my arrival, but I could see most people were here and massing around a larger tent which I took to be the mess tent. I joined them and a porter thrust a mug of steaming hot chocolate into my hand. Frank was being greeted, he looked out on his feet, and although one or two were clapping him on his back, it was evident he was in some distress.

Looking back down the mountain, Hualca was just making it into the water meadow with Debbie. She was almost overcome with joy on reaching us, but there were tears in the group, and between us that night we polished off two bottles of rum Hualca had thoughtfully brought along.

Later, in the early hours I experienced my first ever bout of what I have come to call my Night Najjers. It occurs only at altitude and involves the body being asleep, but the brain being far too awake for my own good and having wild imaginings of nightmarish proportions which seem to go on until dawn. I've imagined tiger attack in the Himalayas, being swallowing by landslide in the Atlas, terrible vertigo on Kilimanjaro and here death by freezing. Great fun this adventuring.

My diary entry describes my mood;

"Pre-dawn, still in sleeping bag, fully clothed with woolly hat

and socks. Frogs been calling all night, now joined by dawn chorus. Because of breath-jerks (sic), first sleep for 3 nights, but very uncomfortable under canvas. This Inca trail is tough. Interminable strength sapping climbs which steal your breath leaving you physically wrecked. But you must go on! A five-minute rest then mental turmoil when within 20 steps you have to stop again. The pounding descents leave legs like jelly and the sickening knowledge that going down means an up will surely follow. This climb to Dead Woman's Pass has been sheer hell, arriving at camp so high that the biting winds caused ice-encrusted tents. Thank God for the rum and hot water bottles!"

At dawn a bowl of hot water with soap was put outside the tent alongside a huge mug of coca tea. I'd avoided the leaves as far as possible, but on this occasion succumbed to the mild narcotic.

Breakfast in the mess tent was scrambled eggs, porridge and jam; or jelly as the Americans insist on calling it. Hualca warned us of another difficult early climb, after which the conditions would ease.

So it was that after an hour's hard work we reached the highest point, 4,250 metres, nearly 14,000 feet, congratulated each other and then spent the next couple of days zig-zagging around the Andes, following the main path used by the Inca to join Cusco to Machu Picchu and the jungle of the Amazon basin beyond. The views across the mountain range which included four of the highest peaks in South America (Aconcagua, the highest at 6,962 metres, is in Argentina) were never less than spectacular; high, jagged peaks covered in glaciers. It was no wonder, as Hualca assured us, that the Inca saw so much religious significance in the mountains reaching up to the sky and therefore the gods.

We had makeshift toilets at the camps, and Debbie confided she never closed the doors. "What a view to pee to" she enthused.

There were detours. One to a valley known for condors, we

saw two at a distance. Hualca told us they were monogamous, could live for 70 years, only ever raise one chick, and when their partner dies, the remaining bird soars to a great height then plummets head first into the ground. I imagined some of this is true, and some the mythology that surrounds these great creatures. Either way, the condor is a huge vulture.

Other visits off the trail took us to garrison settlements or signal posts; outlying living quarters of the Inca, and no doubt, pre-Inca regiments. Similar to Olluntaytambo, these include more clambering.

On our second night under canvas Frank asked the porters to erect his tent in the next valley, aware that his snoring was keeping people awake. It is a tribute to his sonorous strength that it made no difference.

Our third and final camp was at a communal site where all trekkers meet up before arrival at the city. It was a little disappointing to be back in a form of civilisation (it was noisy and had a pub), but the emphasis was on the final assault beginning at 3:45 am. Not long in bed when the storm broke; torrential rain, thunderclaps and lightning which lit up the tent like a camera flash. Quite disconcerting, and impossible to sleep.

The storm eventually cleared, we greeted the morning and the excitement was tangible as we quickly breakfasted and intended to reach the Sun Gate, heralding the entrance to the city, at dawn. There was an hour's interesting trek with head torches. The problem this created was that whenever you spoke to someone, or reacted to someone speaking to you, you blinded each other. Finally, we had to climb 52 huge steps, and we were there.

It was disappointing to broach the Sun Gate to find that the cloud had dropped again and we were in heavy drizzle with poor visibility. These things happen, that's why it is called a cloud forest. We trekked solemnly down to the city, and when just above, the clouds cleared and we had our first view of this wonderfully preserved city sitting in the saddle, backed by the Picchu mountain, flanked by two valleys and surrounded by heavily jungled slopes. A true "Wow" moment. I hung my cagoule up to dry and the exploration of this magical, mystical place could begin.

Hualca gave us the tour, showing us the various temples, explaining how it was constructed and pontificating on the meanings of a variety of architectural oddities. It was strange after three days in the mountains to be surrounded by tourists. When Hualca had finished his animated and enthusiastic explanations I had two hours free to explore the place for myself, and I filled every second.

There are many theories about Machu Picchu, but the Inca never recorded their history. The Spanish priests which followed the conquistadores were the first to document the Inca story, but their knowledge was probably apocryphal. There are many questions still to address; Who built it, for what purpose, why when well-hidden was it abandoned, why was it allowed to return to the jungle, what happened to all the gold, and how could it all have happened in just 100 years?

I didn't realise at the time that one day I would be able to return and try to answer those imponderables.

Our day in Machu Picchu completed, we left the ruins and took a bus down to the railhead, the only other way to reach M.P., to discover a little town called Aguas Calientes, just a few shops and restaurants which had grown around the railway station. After some lunch we took the train, which follows the Urubamba river valley, back to Olluntaytambo where a minibus was waiting to return us to Cusco and our hotel. It was gone dark by our arrival so we dined fairly quickly and took to our beds gratefully after three nights on hard mats. During this final meal Hualca confessed to me he had a younger brother his parents had given the same name but substituted the "L" for an "N". In his village and their school, he had made sure it had been the subject of constant amusement.

Morning flights took us back to Lima and the group dispersed to its various countries. Some, of course, were going on to further adventures. I had to be back in Blighty by Monday, but it still allowed me enough time to enjoy an afternoon with Debbie in the salubrious Lima suburb of Miraflores, where the shops, bars and restaurants are built into the cliffs overlooking the Pacific Ocean, and where you can drink beer and watch the surfers catching the waves or the hang gliders flying the thermals.

That evening Debbie flew to Belize where she had bought a house on the Caribbean, and I flew to Birmingham as I was teaching year ten the advantages and disadvantages of limited liability.

Lima, again.

For the next 14 years it rankled with me that I had been to Peru and missed Lake Titicaca. And then I had the opportunity to join an expedition which would be doing just that, as well as flying over the Nazca Desert. Plus, it would be visiting Macchu Picchu, by train. Well, I do have a policy of "never go back", but I supposed that in this case I could make an exception. The ghosts that I left there wouldn't be missed, apart from Deb; she was a good sort, and Snoring Frank of the huge moustache and Jane: who could forget her and her long suffering Sam.

This time I left the UK in Autumn and arrived in Peru in Springtime. Roger (We are Inca, my mother refused to give me a Saint's name) another short, squat, heavy set, proud Inca replaced Hualca as our guide, and on a sunny afternoon in Miraflores, the posh suburb of Lima, drinking beer, watching the surfers and hang gliders, I began to get to know my fellow travellers. Two young Mancunians: Ruth who lived in Bristol and worked in London and Geneva for DEFRA, which for one strange moment I misheard as Death Row; Georgina who worked in music and with children with learning difficulties and was a self-confessed white witch ("Although I wouldn't call myself that!"), and Helen, a Geordie living and working in an office in York. I'm not allowed, for purposes of propriety to hazard a guess at their ages. Suffice is to say that I was very much a father figure.

We would meet Richard and Andrew; two Londoners and Natalie and Celia; Kiwi sisters, later at dinner.

I soon had an opportunity to show my companions the sod's law of travelling which tends to accompany my gallivants. We chose a little restaurant off the main street for lunch in the hope of authenticity and better value for money. I ordered a pizza (how authentic?), "Hawaiiana" appeared to be the Spanish for Hawaiian, so, ham and pineapple. It looked slightly strange when it arrived on a wooden chopping board "No jamon, tiene melocoton" explained the Señora. That's OK, I like peaches, they go well with pineapple!

As I tucked in I discovered something a little chewy, which on investigation were bits of paper; the price tag and bar code from the chopping board which, now disintegrated, had become another part of my pizza.

"There's no problem," I explained to my fellow diners, "these things just happen. It's serendipity, all part of life's rich tapestry. It's just that it does tend to follow me around." We were to discover that Ruth is a fellow sufferer.

Ruth holds a doctorate in theologian history, and has missed her vocation; which naturally is teaching theologian history. Instead she advises farmers about government policy, and travels. We soon discovered she has two left feet, which isn't too bad as she is left handed, but can't throw a dart (well, she can, she just can't hit a dartboard), wield a pool cue (she'd be better off using the blunt end) or play table football (a habitual spinner).

For dinner we were recommended a backpackers' restaurant which was both cheap and authentic. I chose the Ceviche, a real Peruvian dish of raw fish marinaded in chillis and citrus juice.

"Que es el pescado del dia?" I ventured.

"Hoy es marlin" the waiter assured as he served the ice cold Cusquena beers. Sounds good I thought, nice firm white fish.

Sadly, the fish ranged from mushy to chewy, a texture that I discovered was almost vomit-inducing, so I placed ceviche in my culinary room 101, somewhere alongside sushi.

Still, the salad was tasty and spicy, and the beer and company agreeable. Everyone was thrilled to learn I had been to Peru and Machu Picchu before, and were keen to pick my brains.

The next day we were bussing it to Nazca, a six-hour journey and I was able to put everyone at ease assuring that the inter city buses of South America are much better than the more infamous chicken buses which operate locally.

Indeed, after a splendid breakfast at the bus station (where you check in as at an airport) of coffee and empanadas (savoury pies) we boarded the "Cruz del Sur" double decker. Up the four stairs and turning left, it was like being in the first class compartment of an airliner. The deep, wide leather seats tilted to a very comfortable angle, and there were attachments to the seats in front which you lowered to rest your whole legs. There were individual televisions in the seat backs, personal headphones, and an excellent complimentary refreshments service.

Thus we entered the bustle of Lima's rush hour, and it was a good hour before we were clear of the choking inner city avenues of shops, malls, offices and restaurants; then passing industrial estates and suburbs, and finally alongside the sprawling, higgledy-piggledy, tin-roofed shanty town communities known as Favelas. Eventually we were clear and heading south on the Pan American Highway. We appeared to travel down a fertile plain, with the Pacific Ocean crashing onto the beaches to our right, and the Andes mountains rising beyond to our left. Every so often there would be a colourful community of condominiums in various stages of construction to drive through. Each had their associated billboards advertising properties guaranteeing family seaside bliss from only a hundred or so thousands of Soles. Thus we were quite quickly a whole continent away from the inhabitants of those Favelas.

In our air conditioned luxury liner, we watched the scenery and dozed. I introduced Ruth to Simon and Garfunkel's road song where Paul is looking for America with Cathy. Laughing on the bus, we snuggled down under our blankets.

Nazca

Presently we turned left and began to rise up into the desert hills. We had crossed several arid ranges of hills when we suddenly descended a series of precarious hairpin bends down into the Ica Valley, a beautiful, fertile, verdant oasis fed by the meltwaters off the Andes. Rising out of the valley we were soon into desert conditions again, and eventually found ourselves on a huge, almost flat plain. The ground was light grey, with no plant life, and a scattering of small to medium boulders. This was a stony desert plateau and a sign soon told us we were in an area of special scientific interest, Las Linas de Nazca, and insisted there was to be no trespassing. I was really keen to see these phenomena from the ground, but since 1975 only archaeologists have been allowed to set foot on this protected plateau.

Around 4pm, after about 300 miles we left our air conditioned coach and walked the 100 yards to the Oro Viejo hotel in a hot, dry 25 degrees. There was a little time available to relax in the gardens and take a swim before sundown. Later, following an acceptable filet mignon, I strolled into the town square, which was full of local families enjoying a balmy evening, but there was no music, and very little party atmosphere. I took to my bed feeling rather subdued.

The Nazca lines are mysterious. When, how and why they were created has been the subject of debate for decades and there are many hypotheses. I'll try to make sense of them as I see it.

Over an area of over 150 square miles of arid plateau are

thousands of straight lines going in various direction, and criss-crossing haphazardly. These are amazing since the creation of a straight line is quite a feat of engineering. But there is more. There are a variety of giant geometric shapes, again hugely difficult to create without theodolites, etc. But there is even more. There are, drawn into the desert, about 70 figures of animals, birds, flowers and others, between 50 and 400 yards long.

They are wonderfully preserved, because, similar to the great pyramids of Giza, there is minimal erosion here from wind or rain. They were created around the time of Christ by a pre-Inca civilisation known as the Nazca people. These people most likely designed and produced them using ropes and stakes, and the removal of the top stones. The probable use of them as ceremonial walkways, would have then cemented their existence. And their purpose was almost certainly religious; messages for their gods. Or could they have been for art; the simple, human pleasure of creating artefacts (as in; if we don't have caves, where do we put our drawings?). Or perhaps as I have pontificated about the Great Wall of China, they were a way of keeping idle hands and minds busy, away from ideas of insurrection or escape.

Whichever, I would soon be given the opportunity to admire and study them first hand. I'm flying over them at dawn.

We are a party of 12, which is useful as we are led, on a beautiful sunny morning, over the tarmac to a 12 seater single propeller Cessna. We'd been individually weighed in the tiny terminal building, but the pilot ignores that and just looks at us and allocates each to either side of the aircraft. Manuel, our smiling pilot with long black curly hair, is one of those Peruvian Indians who don't grow facial hair, giving him a very young demeanour; he introduces himself and Pedro, his tall, slim co-pilot who looks a lot older.

"Do not take photographs. You can see the pictures on Google. Use your eyes and enjoy the view. I will talk you through the images. You all speak English, right?"

"Si!" we meekly reply.

"Ok, fasten your seatbelts. Let's go!"

With that he opened the throttle and we sped down the runway and up into the air.

Almost immediately we banked right and he directed us to view the "Spaceman", a simple drawing on the side of a hill, of an upright figure, waving and seemingly wearing a helmet with goggles, and boots, apparently a recent discovery.

Manuel banks the aircraft so that both sides can clearly view the lines and the figures. One of the features I found really interesting was the way the lines went through what had at some stage been shallow water run-off gullies which I imagined to have been pre line creation. But in reality, all thoughts on how or when or why these lines had been created were forgotten as I could only marvel at these phenomenal creations. There was a whale, a tree, linear depictions of a humming bird, condor and heron. There was a lizard, a dog, and a wonderful spider monkey with a fantastic concentrically curling tail. But my favourite was the spider. You could see quite clearly where the drawing began, at the tip of a rear leg, completed two rear legs, then into a large round abdomen, two further rear legs, onto the body, two front legs, the head (including eyes on stalks) and the two other front legs, the other side of the body, then down the rear leg again to leave the paper (as it were), a 50-yard-long, perfectly symmetric arachnid.

All too soon the experience is over and we have landed, disembarked and thanked the double act of Manuel and Pedro. Time for breakfast back at the hotel which is somewhat farcical as the señorita couldn't have been expecting us, was unable to provide any food, and took over an hour to make coffee. We had to source empanadas elsewhere.

I've failed to reach any conclusion but favour the ceremonial walkway theory. I do believe, however that the spaceman figure and the whale look anachronistic, and could well have been the creations of some modern day crop-circle-types.

Later that day I was able to venture into the desert to see the pre-Inca Chauchilla cemetery, and discovered the landscape is nowhere near flat, but full of hillocks and depressions and haphazard slopes, which made the creation of anything symmetrical virtually impossible without extensive knowledge of geometry. Indeed, one of the linear drawings I had seen that morning was of a huge compass set.

The 2,000-year-old graves with their mummified contents wrapped in textiles and returned to foetal position were fascinating, but it was particularly unnerving when my camera went to facial recognition mode as I focussed on the bleached skulls. Wandering the living museum there were occasional glimpses through the haze of the largest sand dune in the world, Cerro Blanco, nearly 7,000 feet high, which looms over the little town of Nazca. There were also bits of bone strewn everywhere amongst the grit and rocks of the desert. All human, assured Roger, rather grimly.

That evening the itinerary threw up one of those features guaranteed to strike fear into the heart of any adventurer; the overnight bus! No cosy hotel bed, nor even a comfy rail couchette, not even a lumpy sleeping bag under canvass. No, just a draughty, noisy, bouncing hard seat, on which it is impossible to sleep because your head is thrown around, you can't align your back properly, and your legs and feet can only endure chronic pressure point pains. You might fitfully doze occasionally, only to be jerked awake by yet another bump in the road, and you know you will greet the other side of the journey with tired, bleary eyes, an aching body, swollen ankles, and another "never again" saga.

Our experience with Cruz Del Sur had given some hope, but nobody was looking forward to a nine-hour ordeal by bus.

I do have my secret weapon, a blow up neck pillow, which I have employed for over 20 years. Funny, when I started using one on long haul flights, people looked at me like I'd gone mad, to attach an artificial goitre to my head. Now I see most passengers using them, and they're on sale in airside Boots for about £15. I still get mine from the Pound Shop. Guess how much?

Arequipa

We should not have worried. The seats on the road cruiser converted beautifully into comfortable beds and I spent the night sleeping snugly next to a gently snoring Georgina. In one way this was a great pity because not only did I miss the whole journey, but it was also a lost opportunity to get to know better our Mancunian witch.

The 360-mile route actually took us back down to the coast, south on the Panamerican Highway alongside the Pacific Ocean, then up into the mountains to Arequipa; Peru's second city is at an elevation of nearly 7,500 feet.

As we approached the city, you had to marvel at the conical volcanos that surround it, as a pink dawn was breaking behind them. The crew had already woken us with a light breakfast, which was lovely as the first thing the excellent staff of the colonial El Conquistador hotel offered us on check in was a buffet breakfast. Feeling suitably fed and rested I set off to explore.

Turning right out of the hotel, the cobbled street was pedestrianised, although the roads making up the grid system running at right angles, were not. There were modern clothes and furniture shops leading down to the main square, as well as fast food franchises and coffee shops. My first impressions were of a wealthy town. And then I emerged onto the main square from its south east corner, and it is magnificent. There is a colonial double colonnade filling three sides, in the centre are well maintained gardens and lawns and fountains, all in perfect symmetry, and dominating the whole scene, the huge, imposing and quite beautiful, twin towered white cathedral.

At this hour there was a bustle in the square as people rushed off to work, but even now there were people filling the benches around the central fountain to pass the time with their coffee, empanada, and newspaper. Many shops have a wall which they fill with the double sheets of the nation's papers. The headlines appear dominated by football, murders and corrupt politicians. Presidents in Peru, and their wives, usually end up in prison!

There is a group of about 20 young women demonstrating in front of the athedral steps. Nothing unusual in this. In fact, in Peru, if there wasn't some sort of workers' or some other oppressed group's protest, you'd be worried. This particular protest is against domestic violence and the sad fact that young Peruvian girls are looked upon as sex objects by young Peruvian men. A worldwide problem, of course, but in a modern enlightened Peru, women feel emancipated enough to feel they can say "enough!"

A teenage boy has walked by them and was now approaching me. With horror I notice he is wearing one of those "Keep Calm..." tee shirts. But the caption goes on to say "... And Rape On"

Before I can be too traumatised, a group of office workers surround and remonstrate with him. They rip the offending shirt off his back and he is let go. He fearfully scuttles into a side street and is gone.

The Cathedral Basilica de Arequipa on the Plaza de Armas, began construction over 500 years ago. In this time, it has been destroyed or severely damaged eight times by earthquake, once by fire, and once again from volcanic eruption. It has a huge organ, impressive statuary and wonderful bells, but better decorated and more ornate structures I have seen elsewhere in the Catholic world, in buildings less prone to destruction. However, the guided tour of it and its museum, and the roof and its bell towers (where the views of the surrounding volcanoes, and the square beneath are stunning), was excellent.

From here I undertook a tour of a much simpler place next door. The Moorish style Monastery of Santa Catalina is a convent with brightly coloured single storey cells on winding streets, alleyways and tiny plazas. At its height housing 450 upper class nuns, their slaves and servants, the place generated huge wealth from the dowries of the families whose daughters served here. An interesting juxtaposition of two buildings from one institution. One using great riches to create a glorification of His realm, the other designed to engage the simple supplication of His subjects.

A quick bite to eat, then following a tour of the market place (great cheeses and huge potato varieties), I would learn the fate of Juanita, the Ice Maiden. I entered the very solemn Museum of Andean Sanctuaries which housed all sorts of Incan artefacts found from the surrounding mountains. The most important and central attraction was the ceremonially clothed mummified body of a young girl which had been found fallen into the crater of the 20,000 foot dormant stratovolcano, Mount Ampato. She had been taken there over 500 years ago at the age of about 14, had been killed and left there. She was discovered in 1995 and subsequently three other children's bodies were also discovered from different times. There were also treasures found with the bodies, so everything had to be urgently moved before the grave robbers got wind. The frozen bodies have been remarkably preserved making them invaluable to science. But what are the tales behind them?

The young girl has been given the name "Juanita". There has of course been much speculation and conjecture about the events that led to her being there. We are fairly certain because of the clothes in which she was wrapped, the treasures with which she was found, the extreme remote location, and the nature of her death, that hers was a ritualistic human sacrifice to the Incan gods. But why did the people of the time think that this sort of, what we would call barbaric, practice needed to happen, and how did it happen? One explanation may be as follows:

There had been a failure of the crops in the Inca empire (possibly caused by the phenomenon we now know as El Nino, which then had a cycle of about 25 years). In the empire capital, Cuzco, it was decided to give the gods a present of a human child in order to try to appease them. A young girl (a virgin) was selected from a noble family. This dreadful decision would have been sold to the family and indeed to the unfortunate girl as being a great honour! The family would be forever favoured, and the girl would live eternally with the gods. We cannot know if a sacrificial death would have been mentioned as part of the deal. Possibly not, the Inca may well have believed that the child could simply be taken to a holy mountain, closest to the sky, where the gods would arrive to retrieve her. After all, the Spanish who conquered them also had faith in resurrection.

An expedition was chosen to take the child to the holy mountain of Ampato some 250 miles to the South. Should the crops have failed the previous Autumn, at harvest, one would expect this expedition to take place the following Spring. On foot it would take at least a month across difficult terrain, and at the end of it they would have to climb the summit. The "Chosen One" may well have been carried on a litter.

On arrival at the summit, with temperatures way below zero, a ceremony would have taken place and a variety of gifts placed at the sacrificial site. At the last meal of the expedition Juanita would have been plied with alcohol and coca drugs to ease her passage through to her next life. Eventually the child and the gifts would have been left for collection by her gods. But the last "priest" to leave killed her. We know the cause of death was a blow to the side of her head probably from a club swung from behind. Death would have been instant. The expedition returned to Cuzco where I imagine the success of the operation will have been determined. El Nino would not visit again for 25 years.

How often these sacrifices took place we cannot know. There have been other sacrificial bodies discovered throughout the Andes, but not many. We know it happened again here on Ampato at least three more times. Did the "priest-in-the-know" risk angering the gods by killing their gift or did the powers-that-be believe the gods had to have a sacrifice? We again face the problem of instilling on this medieval civilisation our own idea of morality.

The Conquistadores returned to Spain with tales of human sacrifice on a huge scale, with bloody altars and bejewelled priests ripping out beating hearts and thrusting them to the heavens to appease the gods. As I mentioned earlier, I think this was deliberately exaggerated to justify what the Christian Conquistadores inflicted on these people. And this example would appear to bear that out.

We'll never know. And we'll also never know what really happened to that tragic little girl.

What we do know is that Juanita, the Lady of Ampato, the Inca Ice Maiden does indeed live on. Her frozen little body is permanently on display in a specially chilled glass case in a darkened room where the gods of the future can look at, admire her and empathise their love for her. Immortal, as promised.

I emerged into the sunlight rather chastened. We ate that night on the third floor, outdoors, under the stars, overlooking the square and the cathedral. I loved Arequipa, a vibrant town living on the edge of the Pacific ring of fire. The next morning, I walked down to the square and sat on a bench facing the fountains and the cathedral as the sun rose over the volcanoes behind. I stayed an hour just drinking it in, people watching, before returning for breakfast. I could have stayed much longer, but I have condors to see.

Chivay

We have commandeered a minibus and driver for the next few days to take us to Puno via Chivay. Chivay is at the head of the Colca valley, the second deepest gorge in South America, and reputedly deeper than the Grand Canyon. The journey through the sprawling suburbs of Arequipa took a good hour and slightly tainted my rose-tinted view of the city, but climbing out of it we soon came upon the Altiplano, the high plains, and from here we had great views of the mountains beyond, several of which were puffing away.

This high plain created where the Andes are at their widest, is characterised by a bleak, rolling, treeless landscape, green through grasses, mosses and lichen, with occasional salt flats and shallow lakes. Rocky outcrops are weirdly misshapen through wind erosion and on every horizon rise conical mountains, most of them live volcanoes, hence the continuous eruptions. Cities like Arequipa gained their wealth through mining of copper, silver, zinc, tin, lead and other mineral ores. The occasional rusted rail tracks and ghost towns we pass are evidence of the decline of these industries. Farming is now the largest activity here and we pass herds of Llama and Alpaca, which are domesticated, intermingled with the smaller, more skittish Vicuña, which are not. The most colourful aspect of the whole region are the pink flamingos which share the wetlands with other ducks and geese. Altogether a fascinating drive where sometimes the straight road had its vanishing point far, far away into an indeterminate distance.

Thankfully there were lots of lay-bys to stop for refreshments and an opportunity to purchase alpaca woollens; to take selfies with the woolly celebrities and to spot birdlife. Also at miradors there were panoramas of significant mountains with their heights signposted.

In the late afternoon we began our zig-zagging descent from the Altiplano down into the town of Chivay, gateway to the Colca Canyon.

I now became aware of canyon snobbery. It is a little like waterfalls which can be measured by width or depth or height or volume, dependant on creating the title "greatest waterfall". So it is with canyons. "At 3,270 metres deep, Colca is nearly a mile deeper than the Grand Canyon" claimed Roger, proudly.

Well, apart from mixing imperial and metric measurements, there really can be no comparison. Here, the breadth and majesty is nowhere near that created by the Colorado river. It is as green as the largest green canyon in the world - Blyde

River Canyon in South Africa - but again not as picturesque, and it is not as wild and arid as the great Wadi Ghul of Oman. Colca Canyon is indeed very beautiful and impressive, but it does not need to be in any competitive comparison game. It has high mountains, lovely little ancient villages, terraced hillsides and wonderful views, and is indeed a very impressive river valley (there is a difference between valley and canyon?), but what it does have which is unique to this canyon and indeed to this mountain range is the condor.

Meanwhile we are at the head of the valley in the charming colonial town of Chivay, and after checking into the peaceful retreat called Pozo del Cielo hotel, I have a walk around the town. In architecture and layout, a tiny, simpler version of Arequipa, but I loved the statuary at all four corners of the main Plaza, life sized and colourful action statues of Inca Indians. In the indoor marketplace vendors were tucking into early dinners of chicken in soup with rice and on the wall one of the strangest murals I have ever seen. It was a picture of a Peruvian peasant woman in full national dress with a background of meadows and mountains. But they have given her the face of Juanita the Ice maiden, who is beautiful in her correct surroundings, but here, with her teeth protruding through shrunken lips, no nose, black holes for eyes and her frozen and bleached complexion she looks more like the ice hockey goal minder's mask made famous by Friday the Thirteenth's Jason...in colourful skirts and Montera hat.

A couple of miles north of the town are La Calera, the hot thermal springs of Chivay, and I spent a very pleasant couple of hours relaxing in a genuinely hot bath amazed that the usual smell of sulphur had been so successfully filtered out. As we floated and bobbed and chatted with the steep mountains as a backdrop I pontificated on the nature of culinary specialities. Everywhere in the world you go there are specialities on the menu which are a must to try. I have done, and have usually been just a little disappointed, and it was only now as I chatted with other seasoned travellers, that I was beginning to realise why.

Lomo Saltado is stir fried beef, but a goulash is much better; Aji de Gallina is a creamy chicken dish but the supreme or chasseur is preferable, and so it goes on, even down to Cuy, the guinea pig, a bony and slightly shameful substitute for chicken.

So we concluded as our skins became pinker in the hot waters that if foreign specialities were better than other dishes, then they would already have found themselves on internationally renowned menus, instead of being stuck in their own parochialness. For proof, see lasagne, paella, moussaka, boeuf bourgignon, those mentioned above, and even, dare I mention it, pizza. But without peaches and bar code stickers, about which my travelling companions continue to tease.

I returned to the peaceful Pozo del Cielo (Well of the Sky) to witness one of the most beautiful sunsets ever from my west facing window. As the sun sank behind the mountains and the sky turned blood red, the plume from an erupting volcano rose high into the sky and gradually levelled off with the prevailing wind and travelled south into the foreground of the rose pink curtain. My words do the vista a disservice.

The evening was unfortunate. Roger took us to one of those events put on solely for tourists which involved a fairly cheap and uninteresting three course meal (watery soup followed by Aji de Gallina followed by flan), but large bottles of Cusquena. As we ate, a local group in local dress played local songs (El Condor Pasa was third in), then there was a display of local dancing, then the very embarrassing process of dragging up poor unfortunates with two left feet, and watching them bump and grind in a hopeless display of being made a fool of. There was one saving grace. One of the dancers dressed as a condor, complete with sweeping wings and feathered head. Sadly, the condor isn't the prettiest of birds, and the headdress matched it perfectly. Equally sadly, the vision of this "bird" must have been severely impaired as it was knocking people all over the place, which I found highly amusing, having feigned a leg injury to get out of the ritual humiliation. Poor Ruth wasn't so amused. The hooked beak managed to give her both a bruised forehead and a bloody nose in two separate clashes. When she came back from the loo looking like she'd had two rounds with Mike Tyson we also noted a large bruise on her cheek, but said nothing, surmising she'd suffered enough. The next day she rebuked us for not pointing out where she had smudged her make-up.

Barely had dawn broken and we had checked out and on the minibus heading for El Cruz del Condor, a bumpy 30 mile trip up the valley past villages and farms, gradually getting higher and higher until we reach the spot. There were about 50 minibuses and coaches already arrived, some had left Arequipa at three that morning. Stalls were set up selling everything from homemade ice cream to thermal socks, and a line of people stood at the edge of the canyon, patiently looking into its depths and across to its green heights, waiting for condors.

After a fruitless hour I left my particular vantage point. I wandered down to the right to where they waited on a purpose built platform, waited a few minutes then wandered back up to the left, west, in the direction of the deepest part of the gorge, until I was the endmost person in the whole line.

I think I was the first to hear the plaintiff warbled cry, not too dissimilar to the buzzards which circle over my Cannock Chase. And I knew she was below us. She appears from below the mound, clear black, brown and white.

"There!" I shout and point, and all eyes follow. There is an audible "Aaah!", more alleviating the frustration, an expression of relief. It has been a long way to come. We watch as she swoops and glides and flies further west and out of sight. But I'd heard a second wail, and another bird shows, bigger than the first, and he entertains, at one point directing his ten-foot wingspan to almost touching point above me. Then they are two again, swooping and gliding on the thermals, and I and the assembled throng can feel fully indulged.

We had a more relaxed journey back down the valley, stopping at several miradors and a particularly pretty village called Mapa. There was a small white church and several typical statues around the plaza, and locals turned out for photo opportunities. I couldn't resist asking one beautifully adorned mother and daughter and baby llama, "Como se llama .... llama?"

"Bambi," came the reply. I didn't ask what had happened to mum!

Before Chivay we turned right and climbed out of the valley back onto the Altiplano, retracing the journey of yesterday. We even lunched at the same shack, where today a flock of flamingoes, a 'flamboyance' had landed.

At the next crossroads we turned left and east. I was beginning to feel just a little excited. We were heading for Puno, Lake Titicaca's Peruvian port.

The landscape began to change. The primitive mosses and hardy clumps were evolving into grassland and some arable farming. Among the llamas and alpacas and vicuña were herds of sheep and cattle, and there were more homesteads. We passed through the small mining community of Santa Lucia before arriving at the sprawl that is the university city of Juanica. An hour on and we had our first glimpses of the bright blue lake itself. Then we were into Puno, sadly choked of traffic, and signing in for our functional hotel, the Posada del Reyes. It had been a long day.

Puno

Puno was laid out in a grid system, with the main north to south avenue pedestrianised. It was this we followed after a hearty steak meal into the main square, to be greeted by three marching bands. The first band came by, and this being hispanic, it was not just marching, but marching with a swagger and a dance, lots of trumpet, lots of drum. Lines of fancy dressed followers danced behind, there didn't appear to be any theme, just exuberance, and jester types ran around the outside letting off firecrackers. The atmosphere was simple; just fun. Two more bands followed, just the same, wild, tango type tunes, latino movement, laughter and fireworks, then they all gradually disappeared, dancing in the direction of the lake.

"It is merely a dress rehearsal for tomorrow night" Roger advised. Great, by then we'll be on Taquile Island. Perhaps all the islanders will be here.

I dived into a little shop to buy a small bottle of (medicinal) gold rum, very smooth and honey-like. The young man in front of me purchased a two litre bottle of coke and a large bottle of rum. The shopkeeper knew what to do. From under the counter he produced a large bucket and proceeded to empty both bottles into it. He then refilled them with the resulting mixture using a tun dish. Cocktails, Peruvian style.

We had been in the main Plaza de Armas, we now walked back to the hotel via the smaller plaza called Parque Pino. This was obviously for the literati as it had dozens of book stalls all around the outside. There was also a very modern lit church. No sooner had I found a bench on which to sit and sip my medicine than the three marching bands turned up! No loss of energy, exuberance, and no depletion in the stock of fireworks. It was madness.

That night I slept fitfully, suffering from shortness of breath. We are at over 12,000 feet. I was eventually awake and ready for breakfast, and looked at the clock. 1:29. Altitude sucks.

When breakfast finally arrived it included rich, sweet, thick coffee. Worth the wait.

Our first view of the lake was a little enclosed harbour full of brightly coloured imaginative pedalos, evidently built for family fun. Our craft however was a 20 seater, diesel powered ferry, and we clambered aboard after walking down the shopping mall jetty, eager to set off.

Beginning our journey on Lake Titicaca (which means Stone Cat or Puma) there was little to see. The lake was surrounded by tall reeds, and we just chugged up through the narrow channels. After an hour we came to a village and were introduced to the Uros people who live on floating reed islands which they create themselves. One 300 square yard island will be home to an extended family in four or five reed huts. Cooking can be a precarious affair, but there is plenty of water around if flames get out of hand.

It was interesting to meet these cheerful people in their traditional dress and learn how they managed their lives, but the experience was very touristic with the inevitable buying opportunity at the end. We did get a chance however to row their boats made entirely of reed, and I was reminded of the Kon Tiki expeditions of the 1950's where a very earnest explorer, Thor Heyerdahl tried (and probably succeeded) to prove that the South Pacific islands could have first been populated by pre-Columbian American Indians. Kon Tiki was built mainly of balsa, maybe if Thor could have exploited the skills of the Uros people, he may have been even more successful. Were the Maori, Fijians and Tongans descendants of the Inca? The Inca average five foot in height, and do they play rugby? Argument over. And I didn't need to build a raft.

Waving goodbye to the Uros, we were soon on open water and suddenly the majesty of the lake hit me. The sky and water were a matching hue of light blue, the lake was millpond calm, with reeds behind us, ahead only a horizon and to left and right distant snow covered mountains, with the sun almost directly above. We were the only craft on the water.

Lake Titicaca is 5,000 square miles of cold, freshwater. Because we are at altitude, with reduced oxygen, the water is also a very poor habitat for fish. Small orestia are really the only endemic species which thrive and feed the Uros. Most others have been killed off by the introduction of trout. Jacques Cousteau conducted an underwater expedition and concluded the only species of interest to be a large frog. The lake is bordered by both Bolivia and Peru and was originally a thriving waterway for trade between the two countries, hence the Yavari (more of which later). What can never be questioned is its supreme level of natural beauty.

Our destination was the north shore of the island of Tequile, a five mile by one-mile island of dual hills populated by Aymara people who speak Quechua Inca, and specialise in creating garments and bedding. The women create the yarn, the men knit. There are no roads on the island, no cars or motorbikes, no dogs or pack animals, just pathways and sheep and goats. When the boat moors and cuts its engines, the silence is incredible. The water is so calm it doesn't even lap the beach, and there is the tiniest of zephyrs to greet us. That said, it is a strenuous walk up and up, through an ancient Inca gate, up to our simple stone lodgings with a beautiful view across the lake to the south east and the mountains of Bolivia. It is warm now, but we know that at an altitude of over 13,000 feet, it will become very cold tonight.

We are greeted by Bendiguy and his wife, each barely five foot with wizened complexions. Lovely pleasant hosts who are very welcoming but rather dour, none of the smiling cheeriness of their Uros neighbours. They have prepared a lunch of quinoa soup followed by trout fillets with potatoes and corn. Home made cooking, and you can tell.

After an hour relaxing and taking in the views, and watching those zephyrs create the occasional darker blue ripple on the water we set off for what will undoubtedly be one of the highlights of the whole adventure. Sunset over Lake Titicaca.

Cameras to hand, we left the little complex, turned left out of the gate and followed the path for half an hour. Presently we came down to the village square. There were one or two locals hanging around and the occasional giggling gaggle of teenage girls, but generally the phrase almost deserted came to mind. In the grey stone square there were a couple of modern buildings which were certainly inconsistent with their simple surroundings. One was a community hall donated and probably therefore designed by the regional, mainland, council. In the narrow alleys leading off the square were tiny, dark shops run by traditionally clad mother and child.

Climbing away from the village we came to the west of the island and could see the sun had probably an hour left. Each of us found a place to sit, a comfortable rock here, a patch of turf there, a stone bench for me. George began to busy herself and had presently arranged objects and potions for some sort of Druid/Feng Shui style ceremony, and was sitting cross-legged before it. Whatever floats your boat, I thought. However, she also began playing the softest, most soothing music you could wish for, which matched the atmosphere perfectly.

We sat on this green hill, on a tiny island overlooking the calmest most peaceful stretch of water imaginable, as the sun sank slowly and unhurriedly beneath the distant wisps of cloud towards the peaks of the Andes mountains. I have never felt so much at peace with the world. I pontificated that it wasn't the sun sinking, but the world turning, away from the sun into its dark side. It would be easy during such a cerebral moment to lose yourself in contemplation of our position in the Solar System, the Milky Way, the Universe. But no. This was a moment for the tiny blue green planet we call Earth, and to realise that for one brief instant I am experiencing the most beautiful scene our home has to offer.

There was a metaphoric tear as I thought of those for whom this was lost; Mum, Dad, Brother; and a smile when I brought to mind those for whom this will always be a possibility; my grandchildren.

The sun sank, disappeared, leaving a pink glow all around which reflected in the still waters.

As we turned for home, stars began to twinkle in the darkening skies of the east. Back in the village square the temperature had plummeted to only five degrees, yet there was no smoke rising from the cottages. The Aymara apparently, don't believe in heating. They just put on extra clothes and go to bed early. As previously described, dour.

The following is an entry from my diary listed at 4:30am, I don't recall either game:

"Another attack of the Night Najjers. Two beers and a tot of rum, bed at nine, slept well till midnight!!! Knowing it was to be a cold night I slept in clothes plus extra blanket, but found myself fighting for breath and to break out of cocoon. Last night (in Puno) *they* (the Night Najjers) *took the form of some strange Scottish game of joining lines. Tonight it was Verbosity, or something similar; a game where you have to solve a five letter anagram, then the game adds another letter, and so on. Well I was fighting to remember the letters as much as anything. Got up to see stars at 1, then 3:30, now nearly dawn and I'm exhausted with it. No more altitude for me.*

Just watched the sun rise over Lake Titicaca. Beautiful but what a pity due to cold and lack of oxygen almost lifeless. A bit like me this morning!"

After dawn I greeted George as she climbed back up from the seashore some 100 yards below us. "What have you been doing?" I asked reasonably.

"There are some things you have to leave with the Earth" she answered enigmatically, and hurried off to her bed.

I thought to relax and catch up on sleep, but found myself remaining on the warming terrace to see everyone else as they woke and emerged to greet the bright morning.

"Been here all night?" asked Ruth sleepily.

"Might as well have been" I replied, a little too grumpily.

Breakfast was pancakes with Nutella, honey, or strawberry jam and coffee. We said goodbye to our hosts and walked back to the village square we had visited last evening. Leaving the square we turned left to follow the spine of the island south. What followed was two hours of the most beautiful trekking I had ever encountered. There was stunning scenery at every step. Either side of the narrow path were green fields which we learned are on a strict six-year rotation, and for this the island is divided into six segments to ensure fresh crops and rejuvenated quality soil at all times. Around us spread the lake, its blue placid waters stretching to its distant mountainous shores. At the highest point of the island were some Inca ruins, probably an ancient temple as the lake was considered a holy place. The stone gateways were particularly poignant the way they framed the lake and no doubt welcomed the sun, the Inca were specialists at positioning these to frame the solstices.

Eventually we descended and crossed a field to our landing beach. Here was a small restaurant which fed us soup and trout, and we re-joined our boat for the somnambulant ride back across the still, blue Titicaca. So much more than I had ever imagined.

Back in Puno we walked along the dock to the main road. On our left was the famous Belmond Andean Explorer, Peru's answer to the Orient Express, advertised as South America's only luxury sleeper train.

Once I had dropped my bags off back at the hotel I announced I was going in search of the Yavari. Roger insisted on taking me.

"No, it's ok, I'll take a tuk-tuk back to the dock and find her from there!" I assured.

"But I can show you the museum as well" insisted Roger.

"Roger, it's Friday, 3:30, everything is closing up" but he was already punching numbers into his phone.

Outside the hotel a taxi was waiting and after half an hour of scouring Puno's back streets the driver dropped us off at the Peruvian Naval Headquarters. The uniformed guard (the place was quite obviously not open to the public, let alone tourists) directed us back to the dock we had left nearly two hours previously.

Another taxi is summoned and we are dropped off at the

Belmond Andean Explorer. Roger stood looking confused. This was a train, not a boat. I decided to take charge and looked to see if there was a way around the train. There wasn't so I crawled under one of the carriages and saw a door in the corrugated iron shed which housed the train. I prised the stiff, creaking door open, and there moored to a series of bollards was a gleaming, single red-funnelled black and white steamship. At the sharp end I saw in black lettering YAVARI. I returned to beckon a still confused Roger.

The Yavari isn't large, 100 feet only, and from the dock you can see the fore and aft decks, the bridge and the engine room housing, but it is evident there is no-one around and everywhere is locked up. Very frustrating. Then, near the stern (the blunt end) I can see a gang plank. Cheekily I lifted it up and placed it on the bulwark, we climbed over the gunwale and boarded the boat.

I had a good look around, and although I couldn't enter the bridge and engine room, I could see through the windows to the gleaming brass and polished woodwork. Very impressive. Fantastic Victorian engineering and craftsmanship from pistons to wheelhouse, bells to anchors, the whole hull and superstructure. There was a sharpness to her lines. This old lady was very classy.

So what was the M/N Yavari, and what was she doing here?

In 1861 the Peruvian government commissioned two "passenger, cargo and gunships" from the James Watt Foundry in Birmingham, pioneers in steam. Their purpose was to open up trade routes with Bolivia and be an outlet to Europe for the mineral rich region of the Altiplano.

The work was sub-contracted to The Thames Ironworks and Shipbuilding Company, (founders of West Ham Football Club) who had to produce the ships in kit form for transporting over the Andes. Each crate had to weigh less than three and a half cwt's (hundredweights), the capacity for a mule, that is 390 pounds. They produced 2,766 crates plus two crankshafts, a total weight of 210 tons. The two ships, the

Yavari and the Yapura together with a team of eight British engineers were transported across the Atlantic Ocean by the Mayola, and rounded the Horn to dock at Arica in Southern Peru in October of 1862.

Problems with contracting muleteers, an earthquake, and the War in the Pacific delayed their onward journey for eight years (and at some stage there were bits of ships scattered all over the Andes!), but eventually all crates and engineers made the 220 mile journey from sea level, across the driest desert in the world, over mountain passes of more than 16,000 feet, and through the sub-zero temperatures of the Altiplano to land up here in Puno, at 12,500 feet above sea level, where a pre-built jetty, slipway and machine shops awaited.

Tha Yavari (fired by dried llama dung) was launched on Christmas Day in 1870, the Yapura three years later.

The Yavari plied her trade aiding the regions' exports and linking Lake Titicaca's communities until 1975, a working life of 105 years, aided, no doubt by its freshwater clean air home. An impoverished Peruvian economy forced her into retirement, and she would have been broken up if not for the efforts of Meriel Larken who for 25 years has worked on her restoration so that she is now in the pristine condition I found her more than 150 years since her original commission.

She is now a major tourist attraction, a floating hotel, and occasionally her brand new (1914), mighty bolinger 4-cylinder hot bulb engine is fired up.

Coincidentally Meriel first heard of this ancient British built steamer working for over 100 years on the highest lake in the world in her 1960's history class, same as me. Different class, different school, different teacher, but it hit the same curiosity trigger.

But, of course, I found her on a Friday afternoon when everything was closed up for the weekend.

(The Yapura was renamed the BAP Puno and is still in service on the lake as a hospital ship).

Roger and I took a few photos, disembarked (returning the gangplank to its original position), ducked back under the Belmond Andean Explorer and returned to the hotel. Dinner that night was an uninspired return to the restaurant from two nights ago, and the marching, dancing bands were no more.

The next day brought my return to Cusco. A more extraordinary public bus trip I could not imagine. This was a 150 mile trip across the Altiplano then down into Cusco, but with five tourist stops on the way.

Firstly, we are on the Inka Express bus, and climbing aboard was like entering the first class section of an airliner, that is how luxurious the cabin appeared. "Voyages Brought to a New Level" was the bus company's slogan, and their wide, deep, fully reclining seats were a good start.

No sooner had the journey begun when a guide piped up, a little annoying with his "Who is from where?" opening salvo, and "Welcome to our first stop... which is the traffic lights!" boom, boom. This is 7am. He did generate a friendly atmosphere however and his "Put on your seatbelts, you do not want to die!" gag actually brought giggles as well as groans.

Before we had reached Juanica a second guide introduced himself and explained we would be stopping for four excursions and lunch, and insisted we wear sunscreen, "Look at me," he grinned "when I started this job I was white." There was laughter on the bus, as well as a mildly embarrassed groan from some of the passengers, but these were overly sensitive Europeans, thankfully the grand narrative of political correctness has yet to hit South America. Oh, for their simple innocence.

After Juanica we were out onto the high plains and the wonderful treeless scenery of rolling hills with occasional herds of alpaca and the odd vicuña or flock of flamingos in the low lying lakes and streams. We came to a town called Pukara and everyone is ushered off the bus, "You can use the bathrooms here as on the bus is for number ones only" giggled guide #1 who then split us into two groups to be guided through the pre-Inca museum.

Next stop was the highest point of our trip, La Raya Pass, also the continental divide. More stunning scenery of glaciers, and very cold at 14,040 feet. The descent from here followed a clearly defined valley and a very significant boundary in landscape. From here organised agriculture was much more evident as were the more frequent homesteads and villages.

There was a wonderful buffet lunch before the archaeological ruins at Raqchi, a city laid waste by the conquistadores, but even now showing marvellous feats of Inca (and pre-Inca) civil engineering with massive storehouses and even bigger columns which must have once supported a monumental temple.

The final stop, however was a complete surprise. We were in the colonial town of Andahuaylillas and visiting its church of St. Peter the Apostle, and as we were to discover it is no exaggeration that it is known as the Sistine Chapel of the Americas.

I am not necessarily in favour of rich, ornate churches. They are all over Rome, and in fact wherever Roman Catholicism is the major religion. My problem is with the hypocrisy lying at the centre of the Christian religion; a religion which teaches that everyone should sacrifice to aid the meek and mild, the poor and needy; that claims it is easier for a camel to go through the eye of a needle than for a rich man to enter the Kingdom of Heaven. Yet all over the world, there are these temples to His worship and they are garnished with riches almost incapable of comprehension, not only gold and jewellery but also art masters which are worth inestimable fortunes. Yet outside these temples exists the most punishing and wretched poverty. And, just like the beggars that plead emphatically with those entering Vatican City, this is especially true in South America.

But they are beautiful, stunning in their craftsmanship and quality of artwork, and here in this town of Andahuaylillas, in this obscure valley between Puno and Cusco (places most people in Europe have never heard of), I was about to witness some of the most sumptuous opulence in the world. Whatever you do, don't mention the parable of the Golden Calf!

As I entered I was greeted by a priest who instructed "No photographs!" and by way of compensation gave me a DVD plus a leaflet explaining that the "Route of the Andean Baroque", of which this church is a part, generated tourists which creates employment, and tourist income which the Jesuits use to feed children, provide libraries, build play centres, promote health and hygiene, and support many more social projects.

So have they managed to turn it around; turn the hypocrisy of the Church's adoration of wealth into the Church being the source of its own ability to alleviate social injustice? The ends, you may claim after over 2,000 years, actually can justify the means, perhaps.

The church itself was very unassuming as it stood in the corner of a pleasantly shaded but simple square. There was one bell tower, some sloping terracotta tiled roofs, the main body being clad in white stucco. The entrance was large, dark and cool, two giant wooden doors depicted bulls, once clad in gold. Inside, every niche, wall, ceiling, and corner was covered in blue, red and gold. There were huge masterpieces depicting the life of St Peter, the death of John the Baptist, the conversion of Saint Pablo, and many more. There were Statues of the Apostles and the Virgin, depictions of Calvary, the magnificent altar, the choir and organ, everywhere was magnificent. And the ceiling, although geometrically patterned was absolutely stunning, and you stood open-mouthed and awe struck at the pure opulence of the place. The Sistine Chapel, of course, it is not. There is not the influence of Michaelangelo, nor the depiction of God and Adam and the creation. But this is a truly glorious place of religious art.

I staggered back into the sunshine, shaken by the wonderful

itinerary of what I had thought would be a simple bus journey from one city to another. I regained my seat, and it was a little less than an hour until we reached the outskirts of Cusco. The town seemed bigger to me, more sprawling than when I had been here previously, but that might simply have been the subjectivity of memory. Cusco nestles between mountains, and the suburbs have crept up the hillsides all around.

Cusco

"The people are foolish," began Roger. "They are anxious to come and live in the city, so they cut down the trees and build their houses. But they are on muddy mountains, not the rock that the Inca built their cities. These muddy mountains are too dangerous."

A strange term "muddy mountains", but I knew what Roger meant. Once you take the trees and vegetation off of these hillsides, the soil has little left to bind it together, and a series of downpours could easily undermine the slopes and the next thing you have is mudslides and the desperate digging out of scores of buried bodies. "Throughout South America people build on the muddy mountains," moaned Roger. And every so often the BBC World Service reminds us of this.

On reaching the bus station our guides bade us a fond farewell; "Thank you for coming, we will never see you again!" they both said with grinning and cheeky smiles. We soon found our hotel, the Emperador Plaza, and that is when the fireworks began, quite literally.

We had arrived during the celebrations for the day of the Black Christ, whom I'd always known as El Christo Negro, but now, possibly because of politically correct concerns (PC arrives in South America!), is called El Christo Moreno, the Brown Christ.

I walked with Ruth, George and Helen to the bottom of the street and turned right to see the steps that lead up to the cathedral's north portal. Here were six or seven 30 foot towers built of bamboo. Each tower was loaded with fireworks on fuses to guarantee a synchronised spectacular display. We climbed the steps and stood in front of the main gate where a little old man was fine tuning the contents of his tower ready to display. It was twilight, and the Plaza below us was awash with people as bands played in all four corners of the square.

Cusco is famous for its dogs. They roam in packs, socialising and grabbing the occasional bite to eat, whilst harassing no-one. At night most of them go back home, much the same as cats, but cats are nocturnal, dogs, diurnal. One such labrador-sized yellow pooch came and lay at our feet. We didn't realise, but he was awaiting his cue.

His cue came with the "Pyro" lighting the blue touchpaper. Suddenly there were whooshes, followed by bangs and whistles, and great cascades of multi-coloured flame lighting up the Plaza, and the dog went into what I can only describe as an ecstasy of delight. He was jumping up and down, tail wagging furiously as he barked and barked at the noise and light. He kept this up for the whole ten minutes of the display, and after the fireworks had reached their impressive crescendo, he came back to lie peacefully at our feet until the next tower was ready to burst into life.

After an hour of this assault on our senses we left to find something to eat and drink. On the roof terrace of La Feria Cocina overlooking the Plaza de Armas with its mad, party atmosphere, I looked up to see the lights of the favellas built on the muddy mountains surrounding us, then up to the ruins of Sacsayhuaman to find the brightly lit Christ the Redeemer statue, then up to the heavens and the Milky Way. Tomorrow is the excursion to the Sacred Valley. I'd been here before.

Pisac is a delightful, colourful market town on the floor of the valley. I wandered its narrow streets, darting into hidden gardens, stopping to discover the local produce, and occasionally enjoying a beer in a pleasantly shaded bar.

Later that day I sat at the top of the Olluntaytambo ruins and looked out over three river valleys. Olluntaytambo is variously known as a temple and a fortress, the most we know is that it existed pre-Inca and its importance lay in the three valleys it protects. On the mountains surrounding it you can see the vestiges of terraces showing agriculture to have thrived here for millennia.

Roger pointed east. "This is the valley to the Inca capital, Cusco, from where Pizarro the conqueror came." He pointed south "This is the valley to Vilcabamba to where Manco Inca retreated to lead the Spanish away from Machu Picchu. He blocked the valley north west and gave the remaining Inca time to regroup in the Amazon jungle."

Roger was answering my question, the one I had pondered for years, "How had a force of 195 men defeated a civilisation of thirty million?"

There were many factors I had discovered and Roger had confirmed. The Conquistadores had arrived at a time of civil war among the Inca; they lacked leadership and there was a confusion of loyalties. The Conquistadores had horses, an animal unknown to the Inca, they also had power over these huge creatures which led the Inca into believing these men to be either gods or messengers from the gods. The Conquistadores had rifles, a weapon so powerful it could kill to supply food, as well as providing instant destruction to any uprising. The Conquistadores had an unquenchable belief in their right to subjugate these heathens.

For these reasons, early encounters often led to awful massacres such as the battle of Caramarca in 1532. The local Inca prince, Atahualpa brought 6,000 of his unarmed people to meet with Francisco Pizarro. The objective, it would appear was to negotiate a peaceful future together. Friars tried to persuade Atahualpa to accept the Bible, but amid much misconstrued communications, the Spanish eventually opened fire and charged the Inca, leaving over 2,000 dead and Atahualpa captured where he spent the next few years as ransom for the riches of his kingdom, before being murdered. Some historians think there was a sad and terrible acceptance of the Inca to their fate, but history shows there were many uprisings before the Inca people and their culture were eventually destroyed and assimilated into Spanish colonialism

There were two more major advantages the Conquistadores had which led inexorably to the destruction of the Inca Empire (by 1572, only 80 years since Columbus had discovered the Americas!). First there were the diseases they introduced for which the Inca had no defence. This wasn't some sort of germ warfare, the Spanish had no way of knowing their illnesses (alien viruses) could reap such havoc. It just so happened that with no immunity, the native inhabitants would die like flies. Secondly there were rats; again not introduced on purpose, but once these vermin left the ships and invaded an ecosystem which had no natural protection, they multiplied at a remarkable rate.

"You remember the storehouses we saw at Raqchi?" Roger asked, "They stored the grain and other crops which could see the population through years of El Nino inspired scarcity. They only had to protect them from mice. Once the plague of rats appeared and devoured the stores overnight, the job of the Conquistadores was made very easy."

It is difficult to look sympathetically upon these events with our 21st century sensitivity but perhaps it helps if you imagine that all of the gold won by the Conquistadores had to make its way back to Spain via cities like Granada in Nicaragua, Cartagena in Columbia and Panama City, and most of it was robbed by British buccaneers like Drake and Morgan. What did make it to Spain went into gilding their churches. We, the British, on the other hand, used the gold to finance our slave trade and build our own worldwide empire. And what happened to the South American Indian was no worse nor better than how their North American cousins were treated. Abysmal.

It is one thing to defeat armies and capture towns, but what did happen to the 30 million strong Inca population. Well over 27 million died from measles and smallpox. Mostly children suffered mortality, hindering the advancement of many generations; women were taken as servants or concubines, men who survived the warfare used as slaves. Those who outlived the plagues, collaborated and converted to Christianity survived, as did those few who disappeared into the Amazon rainforest, possibly via Machu Picchu.

Deep in thought we returned to Cusco, where, guess what, they were still letting off fireworks. Do these people never stop celebrating? What a difference half a millennium makes.

The next morning was my return to Machu Picchu day, and you could feel the excitement in the whole group. For them, this was the highlight they had awaited patiently.

We breakfasted early and took a minibus out of the centre, up and out of the valley, and down to the railway station. Seated on the train we chatted with a group of French tourists from Lyons. We chatted about the Midi, particularly the Languedoc and the light where the Pyrenees meet the sea at Collioure, home of Fauvism in both art and cuisine. Then Carcasonne and the crusade to crush the Cathars, Avignon, the temporary home to the Pope, and the Carmargue, the Rhone delta with its black bulls, pink flamingoes and white horses, and my favourite town in the South of France; Les Deux Maries De La Mer.

"How do you know so much about my country? Asked Philippe.

"Oh I've come a long way since I first saw La Route Des Flamants Roses and declared it was the flaming roses road!" I confessed.

After two hours on the train we alighted at the much expanded Aguas Calientes which, for me was a complete shock. Instead of a one street hamlet with a few shacks, a whole new town had sprung up. Now called Machu Picchu Pueblo, there was a town square complete with statues of Inca warriors surrounded by a church, souvenir shops, restaurants galore, each advertising special offers, travel agents and mini-markets. The streets at the back of the plaza led up to more businesses and many hotels. They were steep and narrow but well paved with gullies for rain water, fountains and plant boxes. Only the railway had access to the town (buses parked out of town to take tourists to and from the ruins), therefore there were no motorised vehicles, just electric tuk-tuks to deliver produce. There was also a hospital, school, police station and council offices. The town exists for the ruins, and houses those who work with the ruins and those who service the tourists. People who work here, live here with their families, hence the whole brand new infrastructure.

We dropped our bags at the Marco Wasi Hotel, walked to the bus stop, and were taken the zig zag hairpin route up the mountain to the entrance. Inside the entrance Roger explained we would climb to the Sun Gate in order to get the best views of the city, then come down for a guided tour of the ruins themselves. He pointed up to the Sun Gate and some of the group visibly blanched. "That looks one helluva climb!" gasped Helen.

We set off, looking back every few yards as the views of the city became more and more spectacular. The group strung out and I decided to hang back with Andrew (Londoner, bad knee) and Natalie (Unfit kiwi, not many of them!), or else they would never make it. We'd trekked a good hour and were soaked in sweat when a Scot, David had to pull out. We left him in a clearing where I was due to meet a smug American (unknown at the time) later.

I kept cajoling and nagging at Andrew and Natalie with "Keep going, nice and slowly, 'Pole, Pole', just around the next bend, nearly there", and people we passed who were descending could see they were struggling and confirmed my encouragements.

We made the Sun Gate with the others waiting for us, and sat down on a rock to take in the achievement and the beautiful views surrounding us, and the gorgeous sunshine. I was in seventh heaven, last time I'd been here it had been cold, wet, misty and downright gloomy. I felt elated.

We weren't on top of a mountain, but simply at the high point of a mountain pass, the entrance to Macchu Pichu if you had been walking from Cusco 600 years ago.

Gradually the group began to descend. I was happy to spend time here, but also keen to get back to the ruins. Eventually Andrew (I'd found him a walking pole, the punishing descent would have really tested his knee) and Natalie felt ready so we set off.

Coming down the mountain I had what I can only describe as another strange American episode. We had not descended far when a young man ascending looked over and called out cheerfully, "Hey, Geoff. Is that you?"

Slightly taken aback I confirmed his assumption and he told me he was worried his father couldn't make the climb but people below (obviously Ruth and Helen, et al) had told him to look out for an elderly man named Geoff who had made the climb.

"So if you see my dad, tell him to carry on up, I'll be waitin' at the top"

Two things struck me. Firstly, if I were climbing with my dad, I would stay with him every step of the way, and secondly if I had ever had the opportunity to have walked this path with my father, I would not have wanted to leave his side.

It was another twenty minutes before I came across a gentleman of my age, sitting on the rock where we'd left David, looking out at the city. "I met your son, by the way, near the Sun Gate. He was worried about you"

He stood up and dusted himself down. He was taller and wirier than me, with a shock of grey hair and wearing a tweed jacket. He looked at me then asked, cryptically, "Can you tell me the number between twelve and fourteen?"

I paused for a moment. Was this some sort of wind up? "Thirteen" I said.

"Ah, you're Australian!" he grinned and nodded.

"No I'm not, I'm English. What on earth makes you think that?" I replied wondering why I attracted such idiots.

"Anyway, you should make it up to the Sun Gate in another half hour or so, if you take it nice and slowly, and rest often" I advised, remembering why I was talking to this man. "It's hot, so you'll need plenty of water," I continued, indicating the bottle I had with me.

"I'm not carrying one of those things," he said belligerently, "I have and apple!" And with that he strode off in the opposite direction.

I shrugged and continued down the mountain. Constantly in front of me was the golden city of Machu Picchu, perched on an Andean pedestal, but surrounded by rain forest clad mountains, all glorying in the warm sunshine from an unclouded blue sky. How different this was from my first time; a chapter reopened, refurbished, and now complete.

By the time we had regrouped in the cafeteria the crowds had gone and we had the place to ourselves. Roger gave us the tour explaining this was pre- Inca but there were contrasting theories on who had built it and when. He did point out the various places where Inca contributions had been made, with their five holies of sun, earth, water, mountains and sky, and their three emblems of snake, puma, and condor (representing the underworld, the middle world of humans, and the upper world of the gods); all in a gorgeous warm light as the shadows lengthened.

We strolled and played on the grassy knolls between the buildings, looking down at the Urubamba and Vilcanota rivers, and up to the famous backdrop, the sugar loaf shaped Mount Picchu. We stood with and walked alongside the local llamas which were extremely tame (and used cleverly to maintain and trim the grass) and I was given the epithet "Llama Whisperer". As the evening approached we took the last bus down to the city.

Later after dinner we mingled and drank Cusquenas with the tourists for which this town had been built. I had not seen a more dedicated area for backpackers since the Thamel district of Kathmandu.

The following day was Halloween, and five of us decided to trek to Mandor. This involved descending the town and following the Railway tracks (Stand By Me style) past Putucusi, then along the river gorge where the Vilcanota eventually merges with the Urubamba. We arrived at the Jardines de Cataratas de Mandor, entered the gate and climbed up into the rainforest. I was keen to remind my companions that this being Halloween, we should neither split up nor allow the back trekker to get separated.

"After all, this is where Predator struck and I for one don't want to be bringing up the rear!" I japed. In the event, the only things that terrorised us were the butterflies and leaf cutting ants.

We were however affected by the curse that afflicts Ruth, after we found the waterfalls. She negotiated the stepping stones only to lose balance and step one boot into the water. In trying to extricate herself, the other boot followed, and she stood shamefaced up to her knees in the onrushing mountain steam, laughing tears and shaking her head "Why is it always me!" she cried.

We left the gardens intact and returned along the railway tracks telling cheese jokes (what cheese is made backwards? How do you hide a horse? How do you eat cheese in Wales? Etc.), ultimately arriving at MPP for the train to Ollantaytambo, and minibus to Cusco where families crowded the Plaza, children dressed in macabre costumes, bands played, and, guess what; fireworks noisily lit up the sky. (Edam, Mascarpone and Caerphilly)

Across the street from the Emperazador hotel was a sports bar where we would meet for a beer before dining. On this night we met a delightful French family from Cahors. "Ah, the city of the black wine," I shamefacedly showed off my local knowledge again. But mum and dad were pleased we knew of their home town and produced a magnum of the dark red wine for which Cahors, in the South West Lot district, is famous. We all took a glass and spent a little time chatting with them and playing with their two boys, aged about eight and ten, on the dartboard, the pool table and the table football.

We left to go to a favourite restaurant of Roger's, and to toast our goodbyes. This would be our last night together as a group.

We returned to the sports bar about ten o'clock to find the French couple thoroughly sozzled and embarrassingly staggering amongst the customers and staff declaring their undying love for all and sundry, whilst they ignored their two boys who were running amok, knocking over chairs, tables and drinks, and becoming a right pair of menaces. Oh, the twin evils of drink and bad parenting.

On the final morning I entered the cathedral to see the Black Christ and take part in the service to commemorate the Day of the Dead (All Souls Day as we call it). It was rather "happy-clappy" and several times the congregation were asked to embrace strangers. I found the experience uplifting. Towards the end of the service there was a hymn. The organ began the introduction and the people sang. I joined in in English. After all, it was one I recognised albeit not as a hymn. The Sound of Silence. How has the church consolidated Paul Simon's claims that people now worshipped neon gods, and that modern prophesies could be found on subway walls?

That afternoon I flew home happy to have made the decision to return to Peru. I'd come to look for America and found significant parts of both continents. In this particular episode I'd connected with memories from my childhood, understood the fragility of civilisation, and closed a previously unfulfilled chapter.

*

Epilogue

For this book I have flown 40 times (I'll take the carbon footprint hit so you don't have to), stayed in over 50 hotels (or hostels or tents) and travelled countless thousands of miles by bus, boat, and most enjoyably on foot. I've met dozens of companions, guides, locals and fellow adventurers. I've climbed mountains, forded rivers, swam seas, and walked deserts and plains. I've visited great cities, towns and villages from current and ancient civilisations. I've witnessed rainforests, volcanoes, canyons, and great natural and man-made waterways. I have spanned two continents and two oceans. I have gallivanted through and had adventures in 14 countries.

I have actually visited more countries of the Americas but not encountered enough adventures to warrant a whole chapter. However, there have been notable memories.

On the Yucatan peninsula of Mexico, I have swum in inland sinkholes called Cenotes, climbed the pyramid of Kobe and delighted in exploring the coastal Mayan city of Tulum.

I watched cricket in Barbados at their Kensington Oval, fed pigeons in their Trafalgar Square, and snorkelled for hours off their west coast.

I have encountered alligators in the Everglades and marvelled at the island city of Manhattan, its bridges, its skyscrapers, and its sad and happy memories of immigrants arriving for Liberty and planes attacking but failing to destroy her.

Kaz and I loved Central Park and its "Imagine" mosaic where everyone sings Beatles songs, and the Plaza Hotel for its reminders of Home Alone 2. And we laughed on an open top bus tour of New York. We were in Times Square where many characters gather, mainly to fleece tourists who want selfies with them. At one junction Kaz looked down and said "Hey, look! There's Schumacher." I followed her gaze expecting to see a model in Formula One driver kit. Instead I saw a great hairy thing. "It's Chewbacca" I corrected, and we fell about.

I have also been angered, and railed at the destruction of the coastlines and coral reefs and the flotsam and jetsam of deadly plastic. When will we begin to learn.

It is difficult to pin down, but my most memorable moment in the Americas was watching mother and baby humpback whales swimming and rising to breath just feet from our boat in the Samana Sound off the east coast of the Dominican Republic.

I'd love to take the railroad through the Canadian Rockies, or cruise the East Coast to Alaska, or camp in Yellowstone Park. But higher up on my list are the Galapagos, Easter Island and Patagonia.

Be all those as they may, my next episode of Random Jaunts takes me to Asia.

A final addendum. It won't have escaped your notice that I persist in giving distances, heights, etc. in miles, yards, feet and inches, where I suppose I should do it in kilometres, metres and centimetres. There are several good reasons for this.

First is our own government's hypocrisy in continuing to prosecute grocers for selling apples by the pound or ham by the quarter, yet persist in signposting all distances on roads in miles and yards. Horses measure in hands and run races in furlongs, a cricket pitch is a chain, you can see for miles, drink a yard of ale, mustn't move an inch, and car sales people persist in using miles per gallon as a sales tool. To resist will take every ounce of your willpower, and how much do I love you? Pound of sugar!

We never really converted to metric in the same way we embraced decimalisation in 1971. Midwives might weigh babies in kilos, but the news spreads in pounds and ounces. Inches, feet and yards are the go to measurements in most households, while clothing sizes and recipes occupy a strange universe somewhere between America and Europe. I've heard children describe themselves as three feet, ten centimetres, or four stones, two and a half kilos. There's even a battle when deciding how much rainforest is being cut down; is it the size of Wales, or Belgium? And no-one has ever known what an acre or hectare is, but everyone knows the size of a football pitch. Or do they?

Let us take a look at that football pitch, the same the world over. We learn at an early age that the goal is eight feet by eight yards, there is a six and 18 yard box, and the penalty spot is 12 yards from the goal. For those "Jonny Foreigners", who I believe also play the game, there are the following simple conversions: the goal is 2.4384 metres by 7.3152 metres. The penalty area is 16.4592 metres, with a 5.4864 box, and the penalty spot is 10.9728 metres from the goal. I hope that has simplified things. I'm off for a pint.

*****

The following excerpt is taken from *Random Jaunts Around Asia*, due for publication in 2020:

Ranthambhore...Number 10

Two hundred and fifty miles south of New Delhi, in the desert state of Rajasthan, lies the town of Sawai Mdhopur, an important town in its own right, with a major rail junction. It is famous however as being the gateway to Ranthambhore National Park, nearly 100,000 acres of of hilly, tropical dry deciduous forest, which rises out of the surrounding arable plain like an eruption of Scottish Highland. It is a Narnia of woods and rivers and streams and lakes, of bushland and rocky terrain. At its centre lies the impressive fortress which bears its name, and here roam sambar and chital (spotted dear), marsh crocodile and Indian gazelle, nilgai and wild boar, hyena, leopard and sloth bear, but of paramount importance, and the phenomenon which allows this remarkably beautiful region to remain wild, uncultivated, and protected: the Bengal Tiger.

There are more of these extraordinary big cats kept as pets in the USA than remain to roam wild throughout Asia, where they are still in danger of predation by poachers seeking to sell parts as aphrodisiacs to the sadly impotent Chinese market.

The last I heard, there are 69 big cats in Ranthambhore where a whole tourist industry has grown up around safari and the vague promise of a glimpse of these magnificent creatures.

I was there in February 2007, when only 25 tigers populated the park, and I recall watching televised cricket from my hotel room in the evenings, lazing around the pool in the midday heat, visiting the fort one lunchtime when a Hindu wedding blew everyone away with their cacophonous drumming and frenzied dancing, and five safari drives - three evening and two early morning (so early that breakfast is only taken on the return).

Three game drives over two days had been fruitless. Don't get me wrong, the antelope and deer are wonderful; the monkeys, both langur and macaque are active, playful and a joy to watch; the rattling around the terrain in open canters and jeeps, very exciting; and the colourful birdlife a delight, especially the peafowl whose haunting cry will be fixed in my memory of this magical wonderland forever. But it is the tigers people come to see.

It is my final day and game drive number four begins pre-dawn when the canter, an open top 20 seater truck, picks me up from the Raj Palace hotel. Three couples are already seated, and I leap up onto the bus with another two youngsters from my hotel. Our guide, a tall studious young Indian with spectacles and a moustache introduces himself as Govindra, or just Gov. I nearly touched my forelock and called him Guv'nor, but resisted the temptation. The hotel provides us with blankets as it will be bitter cold before the sun can rise and warm us up. The five-mile drive to the entrance in what is effectively a cabriolet freezes the face and ears as we huddle under the blankets.

This morning we have been allocated a most picturesque zone which takes in an area below and south east of the looming fort, containing three lakes. Dawn is breaking and cockerels crow to mix with the peacocks' shriek, the parakeets' chatter and the babblers' babble, as we pause before entering the stone gate. Gov explains that a leopard can sometimes be seen sprawled along the branches of the trees across the valley. Today, nothing. A few langur, black-faced monkeys, sit and stare as we sit and stare at them.

We entered the stone gate and meandered down the track of a steep sided valley, the sun's rays from behind dappling the foliage ahead and creating long shadows. A long hour passes as the sun rises and we have many spots of sambur, nilgai and gazelle, none of whom appear worried that a predator may be around.

Suddenly we hear the alarm call of a sambar, a low, sharp bark, and the driver heads in that direction.

Rounding a corner, unbelievably there are four canters in a line down the valley in front of us plus a duo of jeeps going up the other side. At the valley bottom, to the right, there is a small copse and word gets back to us that there is a tigress in there with her three cubs. We can see people in the leading vehicles training their long lenses to the right. They have a perfect view and we know they will not relinquish position 'A' for anybody else, even though the park rules state you should not spend more than five minutes with a tiger before moving on.

We stand on our seats, hang on to the roll bars and lean as far right as is safe. Craning out like this with our field glasses, we occasionally glimpse a paw, perhaps a flank, or the back of a head, it is hard to tell.

Eventually, after much complaining, bobbing and weaving, and jockeying for position, a gasp went up, and there she was, sauntering up the track away from us, followed by her cubs. Four smudges in the distance, there and then gone, left into the undergrowth. Everyone in our canter seemed elated. All I could feel was desperate disappointment. After all, our vehicle had been the first into the park that morning, how could we have got so far behind.

The traffic cleared and we spent the next hour trying to second guess her movements and listening out for any more warning grunts. Nothing, just the usual sambar and chital. The sight of contented grazing deer sadly means no tiger! We see birdlife galore, wild pigs, crocodile and one magnificent sambar stag grazing on a pink lake. But no tigers, and it is now 10am and the drivers are under strict instruction, Gov explains, on pain of a fine and loss of licence, to be out of the park.

We returned and over tea and biscuits on the hotel lawn I contemplated this my tenth safari, and my first big cats, a shadowy glimpse from the end of a traffic jam.

We were back at the stone gate by three, ready for my fifth and final game drive. I was accompanied by the same crew as this morning, except that couple number one had this afternoon brought along their 12-year-old daughter, Jemima, who this morning had been too tired to join us. Our allocated route is zone two, where we will mainly follow the ravine of a river valley.

We are in the valley, single track with bushland and a rocky slope to our right, shrub, tall grass and a dried river bed to our left, and a tall grassy far slope on which we can see sambar grazing.

We hear the alarm call. Ahead, no more than 150 yards, and the driver slows to a crawl as we approach the point. All has gone quiet as Gov instructs the driver to kill the engine and we slow to a halt. We sit, silent and motionless when on the breeze wafts the unmistakable sweet smell of death. "There is a kill here" whispers Govendra. "It is a recent kill, and my guess is that the tiger has dragged it up the bank into the bush and behind those rocks. Everyone's eyes are trained to the right, where he had pointed, as we edge forward, and the smell and the flies get worse.

"Er, it's here," calls Jemima, pointing down to the left. And there it was. We were right on top of it, a mature sambar stag with its neck broken, the carcass apparently unopened. Gov now assures us the kill has been made in the valley, the tiger has dragged it to the side of the track, and unable to go further was now sleeping. "He won't be far away. When he awakes at dusk he will go to the waterhole to drink then return to devour his dinner."

We couldn't wait till dusk. It was gone four, and we only had till six o'clock before our driver had to leave.

Other vehicles arrive. Two jeeps stay beside the increasingly foetid corpse as we depart for the waterhole, a mile or so down the track, to await his appearance.

We arrive at the side of a muddy patch which goes by the title waterhole and sit and watch and wait. The sun is now beating down, and we take on water and reapply sun screen. There is weirdly no sound, no birds, nor insects, nothing. Some doze, others complain about the inactivity. I am increasingly aware of the time.

"We'll know when he's on the move, by the alarm calls the monkeys make for the deer," whispers Gov. But there is just the continuous silence in the heat.

"Surely there's not enough time for him to get here," I ask. "Wouldn't we be better back at the kill?"

After half an hour (it seemed much longer) with no breeze, no sound, and the sun relentlessly beating down on us, Gov agrees our stakeout has been flawed and, frustrated, we creep back to the scene of the crime.

When the vehicle is once again on the move, there is a welcome breeze. Our blankets lie crumpled and forgotten in the foot wells, it now seems impossible this morning can have been so cold.

We relocate the kill and park upwind and a sensible distance from the smell and flies. Minutes pass and we hear a low guttural bellow. Is it an alarm call, or perhaps a distant roar?

"It is a yawn" confirms Gov. We peer into the gathering gloom to our left. "There, there is a tiger!" he breathes excitedly.

No-one can see anything, and Gov begins that futile exercise of trying to point and explain to where he is pointing. "About three trees in, next to that greenish bush, to the right of the dead branch, above that rock, look."

"By the gap in the fork?" asks a baffled Jemima.

"No, about three metres above that, beneath the arching bough." People continue to peer through the bush to where they think Gov is pointing. Then they gasp as a paw reaches up, and as quickly disappears, but everyone has seen the movement and are focussed on the correct spot. We are climbing on seats, hanging onto roll bars, dangerously dangling over the side of the vehicle, when a well camouflaged face appears. It is undoubtedly a round head, with fluffy ears, and it is looking at us.

The collective sharp intakes of breath and excited shouts prove too much and he goes down again. "Shhhhh!" is the next comment.

Over several minutes we glimpse him first clean his front, then his rear paws. He gets onto his haunches and finally to his feet. Magnificent. He slopes off behind us back towards the waterhole and is briefly hidden from us again. Then suddenly about 100 yards down the track he jumps down onto the road, saunters three or four steps, to a gap in the long grass, and he is gone, onto the dried riverbed and out of sight. It has been a marvellous encounter, but with little opportunity to record it.

The rules of safari state that we must not stalk or harass the game, so we turn around and slowly head back to the waterhole to await his arrival. But it is 5:30 when we arrive and we should be heading for the exit. Reluctantly that is what we begin to do, make our way back towards the Stone Gate. It means retracing our route. "The tiger we have seen is a three-and-a-half-year-old male" Govindra explains. "He is very likely a son of Machli, Ranthambhore's most famous Tigress; the Lady of the Lakes".

Govindra continues telling us something of the history of the tiger community here including, rather chillingly of park rangers and villagers who have been attacked and killed. We are progressing slowly up the track, hoping to once again glimpse him, but there are too many blind spots, and deep in the valley, the light is beginning to go.

Govindra is in full flow when I suddenly bang on the roof of the cab and yell to stop. The driver slams on the brake and everyone lurches forward.

"We can't stop now, Geoff" says Gov, "the tiger is long gone, we must go to the exit."

"But there is the gap in the long grass, where he went down. Perhaps he has stayed with his meal" I am pointing into the bush, almost pleading with Gov for one more chance.

Govindra wasn't sure and told the driver to edge forward.

"No," I cried again, insisting. "We must back up. Just give us another few minutes."

All eyes were on our guide as he paused, but his were on the riverbed where our tiger suddenly walked into view.

"Ok, we'll stay" he beamed.

Son of Machli sauntered from the riverbed where we had previously seen him disappear, but he was close to the rear of the canter and we had good views of him. Then, almost on cue, he sat down and began to groom. He was posing.

"Oh, he's beautiful!" said one, "Do we know his name?"

"How about Raja?" offered another.

Too twee, too Kiplingesque, I thought, and it came to me.

"Roger it is then. Roger the Tiger." And it was settled.

The journey back flew by. Literally, the driver only had moments to spare. Amongst the crew there were tears of joy, one might also have been me. I was quietly satisfied that I was the one who had made that final encounter happen. Without my insistence and persistence, we would have missed Roger. We all thanked Gov and his driver as we were dropped off at our hotels. The beer that evening tasted particularly sweet.

Why Ranthambhore Number 10? Well this was my tenth safari on two continents spanning twenty years, and the first time I had seen (at close quarters) a big cat.

Shimba Hills, near Mombassa, Tsavo East and Tsavo West, Amboselli, in the shadow of Kilimanjaro; all in Kenya.

Kruger National Park, Hluhluwe Umfolozi and The St Lucia Wetlands of South Africa.

Mlilwane Game Reserve, in Swaziland.

Sariska Tiger Reserve in India, and now Ranthambhore.
Number Ten.

*

I hope you have enjoyed Laughter On The Bus and my
Random Jaunts Around The Americas. My Random Jaunts
Around Asia are equally adventurous, humorous and
informative, and I hope you will endeavour to read them. Also
those around Africa when I can find the time to sit down and
transfer the jottings from my journal into book number three.

In the mean time, if you have any comments about this book,
or would like to ask any questions about my adventures,
please feel free to email me on geoffleo@hotmail.co.uk or
find me on facebook.

I would also appreciate if you could write a review on
Amazon.

Until Asia.

Printed in Poland
by Amazon Fulfillment
Poland Sp. z o.o., Wrocław

55485744R00127